6as

International Needlework Designs

Books by Mira Silverstein

FUN WITH BARGELLO

FUN WITH APPLIQUÉ

BARGELLO PLUS

INTERNATIONAL NEEDLEWORK DESIGNS

International Needlework Designs

Mira Silverstein

Artwork by Roberta Frauwirth
Photography by Sandy L. Studios

Charles Scribner's Sons

New York

I dedicate this book to my mother, Sara Magaziner,
who introduced me to my first needlepoint.

Copyright © 1978 Mira Silverstein

Library of Congress Cataloging in Publication Data

Silverstein, Mira.
  International needlework designs.

  Bibliography: p. 180
  1. Needlework—Patterns.   I. Title.
TT705.S493   746.4'4   77-21189
ISBN 0-684-15169-3

1 3 5 7 9 11 13 15 17 19 MD/C 20 18 16 14 12 10 8 6 4 2

Printed in the United States of America

ACKNOWLEDGMENTS

I wish to thank all the wonderful people who have helped me to research and compile the photographs and information I needed:

Miss Ursula Carthy of the Irish Tourist Board, Dublin, Ireland; Sister Presentation of the Sisters of Charity of Refuge, Dublin, Ireland; Sister Mary Cronan of the Convent of St. Louis in Carrickmacross, Ireland; Miss Caroline Odgers, public relations, Victoria and Albert Museum, London; Mr. David Lloyd and Miss Margaret Richmond of the Royal School of Needlework, London, England; Miss Louise Mulder, director, the Rijksmuseum, Amsterdam, Holland; Mr. Jorgen Gerrild, Manager of the Secretariat Chamber of Commerce, Copenhagen, Denmark; Mr. Henning Brandt of O. Oehlenschlagers, Copenhagen; Mr. Bent Cramer of Carl J. Permin, Copenhagen; Miss Ingrid Roos of the Nordiska Museum, Stockholm, Sweden; Ms. Ritva Elg of the Stockholm Craft School (Konstfack); Miss Gosta Lilja of Liljevalchs, Stockholm; Miss Edna Martin of Handarbetets Vanner, Stockholm; Miss Inga Johansson of the Svensk Hemslöjd, Stockholm; Mrs. Ingrid Arlenborg of the Hemslöjd, Göteborg, Sweden; Miss Marianne Erikson, assistant director, Rohsska Kontslöjdmuseet, Göteborg; Miss Ann Waddicor of Den Norske Nusfudsforetningen, Oslo, Norway; Miss Agnes Zöllner, public relations, Hotel Duna International, Budapest, Hungary; the entire staff of the Kolocsa Farm House, headquarters of the Kolocsa cottage industry, Hungary; Mr. Joseph S. Hayes, New York representative of Kanebo Ltd. of Japan; Mr. Kazuo Sawada, manager, general affairs, Kanebo Ltd., Osaka, Japan; Miss Margot Kneeland of the Japan Society, New York City; Miss Jean Mailey, assistant curator, Textile Study Room, the Metropolitan Museum of Art, New York City; Mr. Vincent Minetti, director, costume department, the Metropolitan Museum of Art, New York City; Mrs. Cora Ginsburg, collector of antique embroideries and costumes; Mr. Copeland H. Marks, collector and importer of Guatemalan textiles; Mrs. Meira Geyra, artistic director of the America-Israel Cultural Foundation, New York City; Miss Carol Tadelski of Coats & Clark Inc.; Miss Pirjo Tuominen, director of Suomen Käsityon Ystävät (Friends of Finnish Handicraft), Helsinki, Finland; and special thanks to my family for their unfailing support and encouragement; and to my editor, Elinor Parker, whose magic touch transforms a pile of typewritten pages and photographs into an organized book.

FOREWORD

The history of mankind reflects a striving for something more than the necessities of existence. There is ample evidence to indicate that the need for creative expression is inherent in human beings, for it existed even under conditions of slavery. In other words, although sewing began as a utilitarian craft out of necessity to provide clothing and shelter, it evolved into decorative stitchery as the struggle for existence eased and the availability of a variety of materials increased.

It is of interest that here in the most technologically developed country on earth we are witnessing a kind of renaissance, as it were, in creative skills, making it possible for people to gain a sense of usefulness in the midst of an economic crisis and providing the opportunity to create things of beauty.

Celia S. Deschin, Ph.D.

INTRODUCTION

Needlework. A generic and comprehensive term including every aspect of work that can be executed by means of a threaded needle whether plain or decorative, manual or machined, and of whatever description the needle might be.

Dictionary of Needlework,
Caulfield and Saward

The needle is one of the smallest tools on earth, and it dates back practically unchanged to the Stone Age. The use of the needle was known in prehistoric times. Although all traces of textiles that might have confirmed this have long since vanished, ivory needles dating back twenty thousand years have been found in excavations at Solutré in France along with other early man-made tools.

Originally, needlework was utilitarian. It was meant to bind things together and to facilitate making clothing and shelter.

The evolution of a skill develops in direct proportion to its usefulness. At first it happens by chance and without precedent. If a skill serves a purpose, there is a constant desire to improve it. Once it is superseded, it becomes obsolete and is forgotten.

The art of needlework did not evolve simultaneously in all parts of the world, nor did it develop at the same rate. In India and China embroideries reached the height of splendor centuries before the birth of Christ, at least a thousand years before Europe produced anything of importance. Yet, the earliest recorded needle was found in France.

We assume that in all crafts traditions of workmanship flourished and faded over the centuries in many parts of the world at different times. Therefore, it is virtually impossible to establish the earliest period when decorative stitchery first came into existence.

Textiles do not have the lasting properties of bone, pottery, or precious metals, so there is hardly a trace of antiquity in this area. The oldest embroideries on record date back about three thousand years—and only because they have been preserved under most unusual circumstances.

It is not known whether the earliest embroideries were symbolic or purely ornamental. The finest and most elaborate of them were usually found in royal courts or houses of worship, perhaps because only these governing bodies were able to afford such luxuries.

During periods of royal splendor, East and West, embroideries were very fashionable. Nearly every article of clothing for both men and women was covered with fancy stitchery and handmade lace. In Europe, ball gowns and coronation garb were magnificent and some may still be seen in costume galleries of museums around the world.

Not all embroideries were for the gentry. People at all levels of society have always been fond of personal adornment. Even among the most primitive cultures special times were set aside for ceremonial festivities when the people brightened their daily attire. Most of the decorations were probably readily available, such as feathers, furs, teeth, and claws of animals, primitive dyes, and, of course, flowers and leaves.

As various skills increased, more possessions were acquired and these, too, needed ornamentation. Some things were painted; others were carved; and still others, in time, were embroidered.

The ancient Plains Indians discovered a unique way to decorate deer and buffalo hides with porcupine quills. Strips of sinew, dried and made pliable, were worked into tanned hides with the aid of a sharp tool that perforated the hide at intervals. The porcupine quills were softened and colored with primitive dyes and plaited over the sinew in various designs. This is a matter of recorded history and it may have been one of the earliest forms of decorative stitchery.

Peasant embroidery, like all folk art, developed in rural areas wherever the needle was known and the people had the freedom and time to work it. It was a simple and relatively inexpensive way to relieve the drabness of homespun cloth. Here, too, patterns were borrowed from familiar surroundings: flowers, animals, geometrics, and religious symbols. Various symbols or marks were adopted and refined, which served to identify individuals or family groups. In time, patterns and colors became firmly established and are still easily identified, even with the many variations that have come with intermarriage, migrations, and so forth.

Because peasants had only the coarsest fabrics and at best two or three colors with which to embroider, the wealth of embroideries and design variations produced by these simple, and for the most part uneducated, people in the eighteenth and nineteenth centuries is truly staggering.

Needlework is a universal craft. There are differences in design conception, choice of materials, and blending of colors, but it all begins with the simple line stitch that is completed in two motions on the face of the fabric.

The line stitch may be vertical, horizontal, or diagonal. Once it is manipulated in any way before completion, it becomes a loop or a knot. When two or more lines or loops are worked in a specific formation to create a shape that produces a unique texture, we have stitch formations. These are known under generic names and can be varied indefinitely with changes in texture, gauge, and color.

Stitches and stitch formations may be flat or raised—factors affecting texture, not construction. The terms *canvas stitchery* and *linen embroidery* describe the fabrics used in stitchery, not the stitches. All stitches may be adapted to any type of fabric; the differences lie in the texture and gauge of stitch, not in the stitch construction.

Handmade embroidery suffered a decline toward the end of the nineteenth century. The reasons are difficult to pinpoint: a change in fashion or the advent of machinery that duplicated embroidery and lace, or perhaps a combination of both. Embroidery became a leisure art. Professional embroiderers were still needed for church vestments and expensive articles of clothing, but not in the vast numbers that had been employed earlier.

The chaos of World War II destroyed much of what was left of creative stitchery. In the years that followed, there seemed to be a gradual reappearance of handmade stitchery. It never really disappeared; it only experienced a minor eclipse.

In 1974 I decided to take a fresh look at contemporary needlework around the world. I traveled to the countries I knew to be needlework-oriented. I visited museums, workshops, and countless retail and wholesale establishments.

In general terms, decorative stitchery is a booming business both here and abroad. First, there are the suppliers of raw materials. Wool from Australia and New Zealand is sent abroad to countries such as England, Scotland, France, and Sweden to be processed. These are not the only countries that produce and process wool for yarn, but they are the largest and they do distribute most of the world's supply. The yarns are processed, dyed, and packaged for different distributors under various trade names. Some distributors, such as Paternayan in New York City, import undyed wool yarn and dye it in their own factories.

Then there is the cotton and linen used for canvas and the softer embroidery fabrics. The largest distributors are in Denmark, West Germany, France, Sweden, and, to some extent, Belgium and Ireland. Cotton and linen are also used in making the embroidery thread that is employed most widely in Europe. Silk embroidery thread is used almost exclusively in oriental embroidery. It is not easy to work with and is also more expensive as an imported commodity.

Rayon and other novelty yarns are not in evidence abroad except for export. Needles, embroidery scissors, frames, hoops, and stamped designs are very large industries that employ thousands of people. Although the most famous of these are located in Europe, there are many subsidiaries all over the world, altogether too numerous to mention.

The manufactured supplies are handled by large jobbers who export them to retail stores. These are the distributors of painted canvases, stamped linens, counted-stitch patterns, kits, canvas by the yard, and yarns by the skein or box. The most important centers of distribution are in Denmark, Sweden, France, England, and West Germany.

Next to the manufacture of supplies, the commercially produced handcrafts are the largest segment of this business. The cottage industries have worked out well for both employer and employee. These are distribution centers, rather than factories, where workers, mostly women, are given parts or whole pieces of work that they may finish in their homes or "cottages." In the United States it is known as "home work." This method has proved successful in many countries, because mothers of young children are able to augment their income without leaving home for long periods of time. Since this system also eliminates a substantial part of the overhead required to run conventional shops, some of the savings are often passed on to the workers.

Some cottage industries work under the sponsorship of a larger cooperative whose purpose is to preserve the original ethnic flavor of national designs (see chapters on Irish and Hungarian needlework).

I have compiled a selection of embroideries representing the best achievements of men and women from all parts of the world. Most of the samples are contemporary, but a few are old and represent a classic tradition. You may not be able to reproduce these very well, but you will have a nodding acquaintance with some of the finest craftsmanship in the world.

Originally, this book was created for those with some basic knowledge of stitchery; therefore, it did not seem necessary to delve into step-by-step detail on every item. If, however, you are a beginner who has never become familiar with any form of needlework and you are inspired by some of the designs displayed here, don't be discouraged. Select two simple stitches such as a stem (page 170) and a satin (page 170) and take a few lessons from a qualified teacher. As you gain some expertise, you will also acquire self-confidence—enough, maybe, to make a *manton de Manila* like those in Plates 37–39. Buy the finest materials you can afford and work the stitches wth special care. If the project seems overwhelming, work a border only. And when you wear your silk embroidered shawl you will never feel like a beginner again, nor will anyone mistake you for one.

Today the world of needlework offers an immense variety of materials and the possibility of developing one's unique potential in what is increasingly being recognized as an art form as well as an income-producing field.

CONTENTS

MATERIALS

Textiles have come a long way from coarse, grayish homespun. The manufacture of embroidery fabrics and threads is a mushrooming industry with important centers in Sweden, Denmark, Belgium, France, and West Germany. **Embroidery Fabrics and Threads**

Fabrics are available from four mesh to the inch to the finest silk gauze that has to be counted through a magnifying glass. Even-weave cotton and linen can be obtained in various gauges and in dozens of colors, and there is no need to tint or dye anything.

Threads and yarns offer an enormous variety in wool, cotton, silk, rayon, and many blends. Colors are spectacular.

It is interesting to note that stitchery around the world is worked almost exclusively in natural fibers: linen and wool are at the top of the list, cotton is next, and silk is used for luxury items. Novelties and blends are strictly for export.

The history of needle making dates back to the very earliest times. The first **Needles** tool for sewing was probably a sharp flint that served to perforate hides or furs, which were then "sewn" or laced together with sinew. This method of sewing was known to certain tribes of pre-Columbian Indians who borrowed the white man's metal awl long before they used his needle.

In 1868 archaeological excavations at Solutré near Mâcon in France yielded an important treasure of man-made tools and weapons dating back some twenty thousand years. Among these were slim, sharp ivory needles with eyes. These are the oldest known man-made needles.

The fibers that were used for thread and for the needlework are gone forever, but the needle remains to show that sewing existed twenty thousand years ago, perhaps even earlier, and that its importance led to the development of a special tool.

Around 100 B.C., with hardly a change in pattern, the iron needle was introduced. The first evidence of needle making in its more conventional form was to be found in various monasteries and other ecclesiastical centers.

Today, the needle-making industry is one of the most important in the world. Hand-sewing needles, although of the same basic type, are more specialized and designed for every type of thread, fabric, and needlework.

1

It is important to use the right needle at all times. For canvas, heavy open-weave fabrics, or netting a blunt-pointed needle is best. Sharp-pointed needles are best for finer fabrics. If a needle leaves an unsightly hole in your embroidery cloth, look for a thinner shaft.

If you are worried that the very thin needle may be difficult to thread, take a second look at the darners. They come in a large selection of gauges, with long, straight shafts and oblong eyes that are very easy to thread.

Needles are the most inexpensive of tools, and so for a small investment you can have a complete line of specialized needles. Don't keep them in a jumble stuck in a pincushion; leave them in their little cases, clearly labeled, and hang them on a board in a handy spot.

If you are really serious about becoming involved in creative stitchery, you must surround yourself with needles, threads, yarns, silks, linens, velvets, colors, and textures. Hang everything within sight and easy reach for instant inspiration.

Through the courtesy of the Educational Bureau, Coats & Clark, Inc., here are photographs of one of the largest and most comprehensive selections of needles.

Needle Sizes/Eyes & Points

Tapestry Eye
Tapestry and Chenille

Tapestry Point
Blunt

Long Eye
Crewel Primary Darners
Double Long Darners Beading

Normal Point
Sharp Tapered

Round Eye
Sharps Betweens Straw
Glovers

Glovers Point
Tapered with three
sharp cutting edges

Calyx Eye
A basic Sharps needle with a
slotted eye into which the thread
is pulled.

Double Long

5/0 4/0 3/0 2/0 1/0
14 15 16 17 18 1 2 3 4 5 6 7 8 9

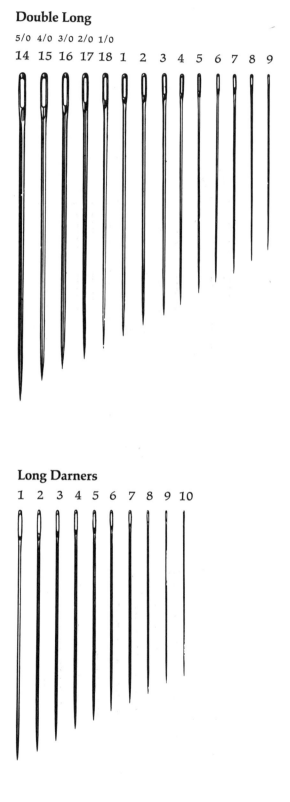

Short Darners

5/0 4/0 3/0 2/0 1/0
14 15 16 17 18 1 2 3 4 5 6 7 8 9 10 11 12

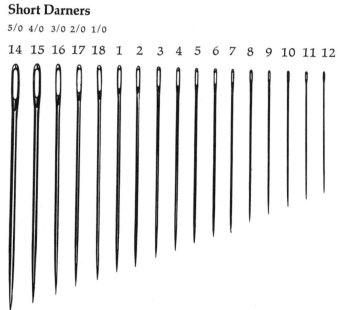

Long Darners

1 2 3 4 5 6 7 8 9 10

Straw/Milliners

3/0 2/0 1/0
16 17 18 2 3 4 5 6 7 8 9 10 11 12

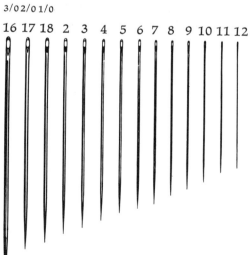

4

Carpet

5/0 4/0 3/0 2/0 1/0

14 15 16 17 18

Sharps

1 2 3 4 5 6 7 8 9 10 11 12

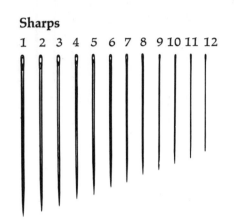

Crewel/Embroidery

1 2 3 4 5 6 7 8 9 10

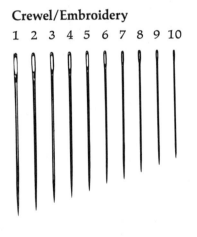

Short Glovers

2/0 1/0 1 2 3 4 5 6 7 8

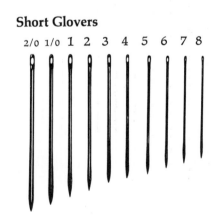

Betweens

1 2 3 4 5 6 7 8 9 10 11 12

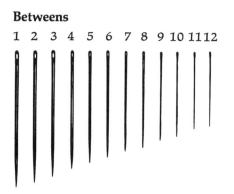

Beading

10 12 13 15

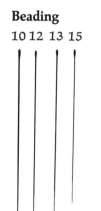

Tapestry

13 14 15 16 17 18 19 20 21 22 23 24 25 26

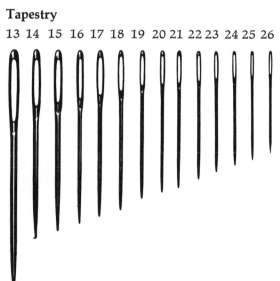

Long Glovers

3/0 2/0 1/0 1 2 3 4 5 6 7 8

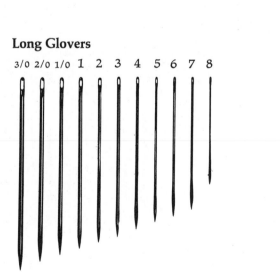

Chenille

13 14 15 16 17 18 19 20 21 22 23 24 25 26

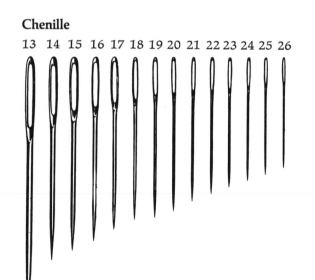

Sharps   Used for general domestic sewing.

Betweens   Similar to sharps but shorter in length. Widely used by tailors because their shortness and strength allow fine work to be carried out on heavy materials.

Crewel or *Embroidery*   Used for most embroidery work. They are the same length as sharps, but the long eye makes threading stranded cotton and silk easier.

Carpet   These are heavier sharps and are used for repairing rugs and carpets.

Beading   The finest-size needles made with long eyes for easier threading, used for fine work on lace, and for beads and sequins.

Tapestry   The extra-long eye makes threading tapestry wool easier. Tapestry needles have a blunt point for use on net or scrim base and are sometimes known as rug or cross-stitch needles.

Chenille   Similar to tapestry needles but having sharp points for heavy embroidery work on closely woven materials.

Glovers   The three sharp edges on the taper of the point will pierce leather without tearing it. Used for glove making or repair.

Calyx   A basic sharps needle with an eye into which the thread is pulled through a slot, not threaded. The second eye in the needle is for providing spring, not threading.

Darners   Long needles with long eyes for easy threading used for darning with wool and cotton. The finest of these are excellent for beading. Their shafts are not tapered as sharply and the eyes are considerably larger than those of conventional beading needles.

Double Long Darners   Extra-long for spanning very large holes. Also made in a heavier range of sizes for especially heavy fabric.

Straw or *Milliners*   Similar to sharps but longer. Used for millinery and any other work for which extra length is required, such as basting.

Below are shown several more unusual needles.

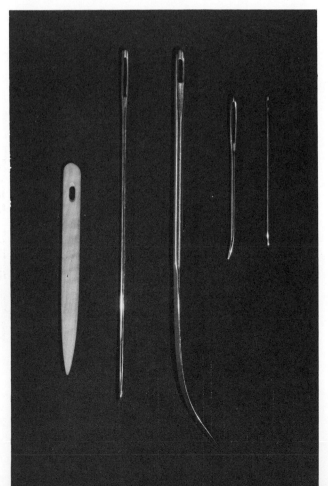

Left to right: a wooden needle from Sweden; a long weaving needle with a ball point; two curved needles for making loops and tassels on rugs; extra-strong carpet needle for sewing carpet backing.

Embroidery frames and hoops are available in a variety of sizes and shapes in most needlepoint shops. Since they are comparatively inexpensive, at least one should be standard equipment for anyone who does needlework. In general, the factory-made frames are well constructed, but they do differ in size and purpose. So make sure that the one you invest in fits your needs.

The round embroidery hoop is designed for finer fabrics and is not suitable for canvas work or bulky fabrics. These should be pinned or laced to a conventional rectangular frame.

It is not possible to list all frames that are currently on the market, but here are a few guidelines that should be helpful in making a selection.

The best frames are the freestanding units or the kind that attach to a table top. They allow more freedom of movement and may be left in place in your working area. Some even come equipped with yarn racks.

Check for adjustable stands and frames that pivot, making the needlework accessible on both sides. Check component parts and pieces. Don't buy anything sight unseen. The wood should be smoothly sanded; and all the wing nuts, bolts, and screws should fit tightly and be accounted for.

Buy the best frame you can afford. The difference in price between a good frame and a substandard one can never compensate for the aggravation of constant tightening, adjusting, and fussing with inadequate equipment.

Occasionally, you might need an extra-heavy frame for driving nails or for string weaving (see page 35). A frame like this has to be custom-made and is one of the easiest do-it-yourself projects in this business.

Use 2-by-4-inch strips of wood cut the length and width you require. Nail the strips into a frame (there is no need to miter corners). Sand smooth and screw metal L-shaped reinforcements into the corners on the underside (see below).

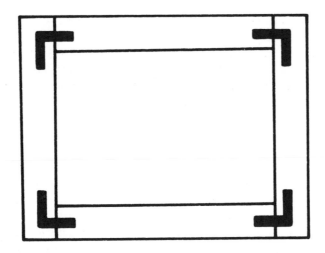

GENERAL INSTRUCTIONS

Enlarging Designs   Most of the patterns in this book are shown in graphs or diagrams in addition to photographs as further aids to those who wish to duplicate them.

A graph indicates a stitch formation. Simply count the threads on the fabric and position the stitches as indicated in the graph. Graphs are also color-coded with different symbols for threads, beads, and sequins, as well as for color placement. To enlarge a graph, you need only to enlarge the stitch size or the gauge of the thread count in your fabric.

Stitch details are shown on pages 170–177.

A diagram is an outline of a given pattern and has to be enlarged to the size of the embroidery. The simplest and most accurate way to enlarge a design is by photostat. This is a readily available service in most cities and not as expensive as you might think. A local newspaper or the yellow pages will provide you with the address of a photostat service near you.

Another way to enlarge a design is by the old reliable method of "square by square." Draw a frame around the given diagram (if it does not already have one) in order to establish its dimensions. Measure width and height of frame and divide each into quarters. Draw the crisscross lines with a ruler and a colored pencil for easy identification.

There should be a grid with sixteen equal squares or rectangles. If the design is complicated, subdivide it once more in width or length or both. Number all squares in sequence. Now, take a sheet of paper somewhat larger than the proposed enlargement and divide it in the same manner with the same number of squares numbered in sequence.

Copy the diagram square by square as accurately as possible. If you know someone with artistic ability, ask him or her to help you. This becomes your pattern enlargement. For transfer or tracing purposes, trace this enlargement on a sheet of tracing paper (see-through paper that can be flipped over for a reverse design). This is very helpful when it becomes necessary to assemble two halves or four quarters of a given pattern.

Some designs are so simple to duplicate that a diagram is not needed. Such designs may be photostat-enlarged right from the photograph or traced on tracing paper and enlarged with squares.

A few diagrams have been printed in actual size and do not need enlarging. Some may fit on one page, in which case they can be traced as is. The larger ones have been divided and printed on two or more pages. The divisions are indicated by dotted lines, which must be lined up as the diagram is traced on one sheet of paper.

Note: Tracing paper is available in most stores where artists' supplies are sold. The paper comes in pads in a variety of sizes and gauges. Select a gauge fine enough to allow a clear view of the diagram to be traced. If the sheets are not large enough to accommodate the design, use smaller ones and tape them edge to edge with clear cellophane tape. Place tape on the underside of the tracing paper, because it will not register pen or pencil marks.

Enlarging Patterns for Articles of Clothing

The two Chinese jackets, the Japanese kimono, and the Bessarabian cross-stitch peasant shirt were not reproduced from any pattern books but were specially adapted here from antique articles of clothing suitable for needlework (see pages 152, 154, 166, and 111). They indicate pattern parts and general directions for reconstruction. The gauges are 1½, 2, or 3 inches for each graph square. This means that the enlargements must be divided into 1½-inch, 2-inch, or 3-inch squares and the pattern outlines copied square by square.

Some dressmaker's supply stores carry a line of special graph paper for enlargements of this kind. The completed enlargement should be made into a muslin pattern to establish personal size and fit.

The two Chinese jackets are wonderful all-purpose tops and can be made in just about any fabric.

The kimono is a standard Japanese pattern and may be used to make an "at home" dress or *yukata*. Shortened to jacket size, it is worn as a *"happi"* coat.

Transferring Design Outlines

Once the design is outlined on tracing paper, the next step is to place it on or transfer it to the selected fabric. Any of several methods can be used for this, depending on the fabric.

For smooth, flat fabrics the most commonly used method of design placement is transfer paper. This is a dressmaker's carbon paper available where sewing

10   supplies are sold. It is smudge-proof and it comes in dark blue for use on light fabrics and in white for dark fabrics.

Press fabric and place on a hard, flat surface. Draw a vertical and a horizontal line through the center with tailor's chalk. Draw the same lines across the tracing with a pencil. Place paper pattern over the fabric to line up centers and pin them across the top. Lift paper and slide carbon, shiny side down, over the fabric and replace paper pattern. Smooth the three layers so that they lie flat. Place a few pins along the sides and trace the design outline with a soft pencil point (not a felt tip). Apply good pressure for best results.

When outline is finished, unpin one side and lift papers gently to see if transfer is clear. Go over the lines if necessary. Unpin the other side and repeat.

Note: Pretest carbon to determine the pressure needed for a clear, sharp transfer; then try not to lift the papers too often before the outline is completed, as this may cause the design to shift.

Transfer paper outlines stay sharp and clear throughout the embroidery and are washable.

If a design is to be used a number of times or if it is a repeat pattern, transferring may be simplified by perforating the design outline with a pin point and rubbing it with charcoal powder. It is the same as using a stencil. Special paper for this is available in dressmaker's supply stores, and you can speed up the piercing process with a straight sewing machine stitch and an unthreaded needle. To transfer a perforated design, place it over the fabric and rub some powdered charcoal over the perforations. Use a clean blackboard eraser and a light touch. Charcoal powder is available in drugstores.

When the outline is imprinted, go over it with a fine felt-tip marker and shake the excess charcoal off the fabric. This is an excellent way to transfer the Indian rug design on page 143, or any other bold pattern, onto medium-heavy fabric. It is a bit messy when used on small, delicate designs.

Textured fabrics, laces, and velvets do not register a standard transfer and must be handled differently. To embroider lace or tulle or fine curtain net, the design outline should be traced on heavy-gauge tracing paper and pinned under the fabric. The embroidery is worked through lace or tulle *and* paper, and after the work is completed the paper is peeled away.

The workers at the Carrickmacross lace center (see page 58) work this method without a frame, but for the inexperienced needleworker I most definitely recommend a frame or embroidery hoop.

Very sheer see-through fabric that is not lace may be placed directly over the design and traced with a fine-point marking pen.

Nubby textures, velvets, blankets, and similar fabrics may be overembroidered with bolder stitches. Apply transfer outline on the reverse side of the fabric if that side is flat and smooth. Outline design with stem stitch, which will show up as backstitch on the right side. Use a contrasting color that will be seen clearly and cover it as you work the embroidery. This works best on velvets.

If the reverse side will not register a transfer, draw your design outline on a piece of fine cotton muslin. Baste it on top of the textured fabric on a frame or embroidery hoop. Work embroidery through both fabrics and then cut away the excess muslin. If any of it still shows, stitch an outline to cover it.

You can use tracing paper instead of muslin, but this is not always successful because paper will not lie flat on a textured fabric. Since bold stitches might require heavier threads, the paper often tears before the stitchery is completed.

These are minor problems, since there are alternatives. Use the muslin patch
method or use the paper patch to work an outline only. Then tear away the paper
and fill in the design with stitches.

To apply a design in half cross, cross-stitch, bargello, or any counted-thread
needlework on a fabric other than even-weave, baste a piece of needlepoint canvas over the fabric. The design may be painted on the canvas or worked in
counted thread from a graph.

There is a breakaway canvas with loosely woven threads that may be pulled
out after the needlework is completed, or conventional canvas may be washed to
remove sizing and used the same way. This method is a nuisance and rarely looks
good except in the hands of a professional. The canvas threads are sometimes
difficult to pull out if the stitches are too tight. If the stitches are worked loosely,
they lack uniformity and the finished work looks uneven.

Work the canvas patch with *interlocked canvas*. It does not ravel and the
threads lie flat. Cut it close to the design outline and place the end stitches over
the canvas border and into the fabric. There is no need to struggle with pulled
threads. Canvas over fabric should be worked on a frame.

A needlework pattern can be made into a hot-iron transfer by tracing the outline with a hectograph pencil. This is a red waxlike pencil manufactured by
Eberhard Faber Co. and sold in most needlework supply stores.

After tracing the outline with the hectograph pencil, turn the tracing over on
the fabric and iron it. This must be pretested since there is no way to generalize
iron temperatures and fabric textures. If the iron is too hot it will melt and
smudge the imprint, and if it is too cool the imprint may not register or will come
out spotty. Sometimes a just-right temperature for the transfer will scorch your
fabric—and that is something to watch out for. If the temperature is right, however, this method works very well, indeed, especially on denims and similar fabrics. The hot-iron transfer will wash out completely with soap and water.

Needlework canvas comes under the heading of see-through fabric and should
always be transferred with the design outline placed under it. A light box can be
very useful in this case. A glass-top table with some lamps placed under it
(minus shades) is an excellent light box. A window or glass door is not suitable
for design transfer, because drawing against an upright surface for more than a
few minutes at a time is impossible. Also, there is no way to pin or nail anything to a window, and tape is useless.

Pin the canvas to the paper pattern. Trace all design outlines with a fine-point
felt marker. Use black or gray if the rest of the shades are dark or if the black is
to be stitched as an outline. For pale shades, outline the design with any light
color. A wide mesh such as number 3 to number 5 should be outlined with a
heavier point.

Fill in shades lightly. Bright colors are used mainly for commercial purposes
because they are more eye-catching, but they are also more likely to run when wet.
So if you paint your own, tone them down. The yarns will enliven your work.

Indelible and *waterproof* are the two terms most frequently used to describe
paints for needlework canvas. The indelibility of an art color depends largely on
what you will use as a cleaning agent.

Dipping in water might make some felt markers bleed a little, especially the
brighter colors. Dry cleaning would remove them with hardly a trace left. Some
acrylic paints tend to flake off, and textile paints will slide off the heavy sizing
that coats the canvas.

Oil paint, the all-time favorite, will not budge when dipped in water, but dry cleaning is another story (often quite sad). Imagine sending your oil paintings to be dry cleaned!

Some top needlepoint shops have their own special blend of paint. This is probably the nearest thing to foolproof, but you may rest assured that the formula is a closely guarded secret.

If you don't have much experience in painting canvas, use felt markers. They come in fine or heavy tips and a good range of colors. None of them is always completely waterproof, so use the palest shades. And don't worry so much about wetting canvas and indelible paints. It is really not necessary to wet canvas—not even when blocking, as you will see in the next section.

When a felt marker stains your yarn, the stain may be removed with a mild bleach solution. Several quick dips and a rinse will do it. This treatment will not affect the colored yarns if they are vat dyed, but it will turn white tapestry yarn cream.

Pretest a small area first. You may find it safer simply to pick out the yarn from the stained area and replace the stitches.

Oil paint that has been loosened with cleaning solvents can be a total disaster. Needlepoint canvas painted in oils should be washed lightly with mild soap, such as Woolite or Ivory Flakes, and patted dry.

A good-quality wool yarn does not require frequent cleaning. It retains natural oils that repel dirt and need only an occasional brushing or vacuuming.

On canvas stitchery allow at least 2 inches all around for pillow tops, handbags, and small accessories unless otherwise indicated. Four-inch margins are required for rugs and framed pictures and at least 6 inches for upholstered pieces.

Note: Pretest everything. For washable needlework pretest all pens, pencils, and transfer papers before using. They must either be completely indelible or wash out without a trace. Pretest threads and yarns as well. For nonwashable needlework, be sure to use at least smear-proof transfer aids.

No matter how glowing the guarantee, be sure to double-check. Chemical composition in fabric dyes and art media varies constantly. It does not take long to transfer, embroider, and wash or clean a small section of fabric. And even if it does take long, the extra time is nothing compared to the heartache of ruining a large and important work with untested supplies. With any guarantee, the most you can expect from a dealer is a new pencil or a skein of yarn.

Blocking Needlework

Blocking is a finishing process that helps straighten and freshen needlework before mounting. It evens and fluffs out the stitches and is recommended for needlework that has not been stitched on a frame.

The best blocking surface is a composition board. This is a specially processed material sold in lumber yards. It does not warp and it accommodates nails without splitting or throwing off splinters.

Buy one that is a few inches larger than the largest work you are likely to block. For anything above 30 by 30 inches I recommend professional blocking. You will also need a box of heavy-duty inch-long nails with large heads, a good heavy hammer, a terrycloth towel, an iron, a pencil, and a ruler.

Outline the original dimensions of the entire canvas (including margins). Draw lines right on the board and place the work to be blocked within this outline. Of the four corners of the canvas, two will be very pointed; the other two, which are rather shallow, should be nailed down first. These are opposite corners; nail one into an outlined corner with two or three nails. Pull the other gently but firmly into the opposite outlined corner (blunt-nosed pliers are a good tool for pulling canvas) and nail it down. These two corners will offer the most resistance and should be fastened securely with extra nails.

Pull the lateral sides of the canvas and nail them along the penciled lines. Drive the nails halfway into the board about 1 inch apart. Don't try to block canvas with thumbtacks or push pins. They don't have the strength to withstand the tension and will pop out constantly.

If the canvas is not badly distorted, it should look square. Always block canvas right side up so that you can notice any signs of stress in the stitches.

There is no need to wet a needlepoint canvas before blocking. Block it dry; then place a damp terrycloth towel over it, and glide a hot iron over the towel until it stops steaming. Don't press hard on the iron. The purpose of the ironing is to release hot steam into the canvas and soften the sizing. Steam twice and let the canvas dry for at least twenty-four hours. This much time is required to stiffen the sizing again.

Remove nails with pliers and let the needlework rest for a day or two before mounting it. If a slight distortion has remained in the canvas it will show at this point; and no matter how many times you reblock the canvas, it will not straighten any more.

If you plan to frame the work as a picture or use it as upholstery fabric, a slight distortion will be straightened out in the process. If, however, you plan to finish it as a pillow or a soft, unframed hanging, square the sides with a template or ruler and mark them with chalk. Machine stitch along the chalk outline so that the stitches will become visible on the reverse side. Use these as a guideline to stitch your lining and cut away excess fabric and distorted canvas.

Geometric borders would be ruined in this way, of course, so it might be helpful to work these on a frame, in basketweave or cross-stitch.

Bargello, cross-stitch, or any textured needlework that has been worked in the hand is improved after a light blocking. Since there is no distortion in fabric, there is no need for nails and pliers. Simply mist the reverse side with a fine spray of water (use a potted-plant sprayer). Place work right side up on the blocking board, and pin it all around with push pins. Stretch fabric only until the stitches fluff out. Let dry at least twenty-four hours.

APPLIQUÉ

Appliqué is one of the oldest forms of expressive needlework. It is becoming increasingly popular with contemporary artists who sometimes refer to it as fabric collage.

In the earliest times appliqué was used to depict a story in pictures cut out from colored fabrics, which were sewn with little stitches to a larger background. The fabric shapes were most important; the stitches served only to hold the shapes in place. In contemporary appliqué, however, the stitches are bold and intricate and become an integral part of the design.

Working with appliqué is fun. A design is established quickly. Large shapes are immediately identified and, from the hundreds of stitch variations and available threads, even the tiniest detail can be emphasized.

The background does not need filling in and so a large wall hanging is not as formidable as, for example, a rug worked in tiny half cross-stitch.

There are several appliqué works in this book covering a wide spectrum of techniques and constructions. Some of the pieces are enormous works of art that are not possible to reproduce in diagram outline. The photographs are very clear, however, some of them in color, so that you may examine and perhaps borrow from the artists' individual approaches to appliqué.

In general, appliqué is worked from a prepared plan. You decide on size, pattern, fabrics, and type of stitchery, in that order, and proceed one step at a time.

The background fabric is selected in the predetermined size with a fold-back allowance of 3 or more inches all around. Unless the background is covered completely with appliqué, it is important to decide color and texture at the beginning of the project.

The choice of fabric is determined by size and type of design and the interpretation of the artist. Fabrics fall into two main categories: the type that can be folded back and the type that cannot.

Lightweight, densely woven fabrics are folded back around the pattern cutout, for which a ¼-inch margin should be allowed. The smaller the pattern outline, the finer the fabric needed to achieve a clean, sharp image.

Heavier fabrics or those with deep pile or texture are cumbersome when folded back in appliqué stitchery. The cut edges may be outlined with stitchery such as chain, buttonhole, closed herringbone, couching, and the like. In some instances frayed edges are left as they are for a special decorative touch.

Felt is easiest to work with because it does not fray and needs no folding back. Coloring-book designs or storybook characters cut out in felt and worked in appliqué with bold buttonhole stitches on printed fabrics make attractive decorations for children's rooms. Glue these on a cardboard backing and frame with braided yarn.

In general, appliqué is assembled using one of two methods: transfer and cut-out, or fabric collage.

The first is the standard method, for which some planning is required. The projected design is traced and then transferred to fabric. Two tracings are essential for this: one, to be used in transferring and as reference; and the other, to be cut into component parts that will be used as patterns for the appliqué fabrics. The choice of fabrics and stitches is a matter of personal interpretation.

Fabric collage does not require advance planning except in the projected dimensions. Fabrics are simply cut and pinned to the background. The design develops gradually. Pins are readjusted and fabrics are replaced constantly. It is a good idea to keep a fabric collage pinned to a wall while it is "in the works." This gives you an opportunity to step back and examine it in perspective. When the fabrics are assembled they are overembroidered with all manner of stitches and threads that serve to intensify or subdue the collage.

Each appliqué design in this book is accompanied by individual instructions. Design outlines may be enlarged or reduced and fabrics may be changed—but with a full understanding of their properties.

BEADWORK WITH THREADED NEEDLE

The earliest beads may have been nothing more than natural materials such as shells, seeds, berries, bits of bone, or animal claws and teeth, perhaps even brightly colored beetles—anything interesting that could be easily pierced and strung or tied together with grass fibers, sinew, or whatever was strong and flexible.

The first man-made beads were probably fashioned in clay or carved in wood or ivory, and glass beads were used almost as soon as the art of glass making developed.

Valuable beads were a symbol of wealth and status. They were carved in gemstones and fashioned in precious metals and pearls by skilled artisans. These have not lost their value after thousands of years.

Over the centuries, however, the commercial glass beads were most widely used for decorative purposes. In the seventeenth, eighteenth, and nineteenth centuries, beads were enormously popular. With the advent of the specialized beading needle, it was possible to work them into embroidery with stunning results.

Everything imaginable was ornamented with beads of one kind or another. Lampshades, curtains, pictures, and innumerable articles of clothing and accessories were covered with beads.

Glass-manufacturing centers in Italy and France exported beads all over the world. Beadwork became a popular craft. The wide range of color and general availability of glass beads had an important influence on many primitive cultures who adopted beadwork in preference to some of the native crafts.

Over the years, commercial beads became coarser and the colors more garish. This lowering of quality had a disastrous effect on some native design and color interpretation.

In the end, plastic dealt the final blow to the fine art of decorative beadwork. The soft shimmer and color range of glass is simply impossible to duplicate in plastic.

Plastic, like glass in its own time, was a marvelous discovery, and its usefulness is increasing. Man will keep improving plastic, and it will be forever color-fast, waterproof, and shatterproof. But it will never replace fine art glass; and so when I see a hand-crafted African drum or Indian moccasins decorated with bright plastic beads I feel a sense of loss.

Today, there is a renewed interest in beads, especially the handcrafted type. The valuable beads of gemstone, precious metals, and natural pearls never go out of style; they merely increase in value.

Mass-produced beads made of glass and plastic are used in crafts. Really fine beadwork with threaded needle is rare and usually an individual endeavor.

I have selected three different examples of beadwork for this book. Two are nineteenth century and may have been made in America (see page 19 and Plate 1). The third is a Rumanian folk costume, also from the nineteenth century (Plates 22 and 23). All three are fine representative samples of beadwork and may be adapted to counted-thread stitchery.

INSTRUCTIONS

    Materials

        30-inch square double-mesh number 10 canvas
        8 ounces tapestry or Persian-type yarn
        Beads (2,000 crystal clear and 5,000 opaque white, approximate count)
        Beeswax
        Tapestry and beading needles
        Embroidery frame (see page 7 for construction)

White Roses Victorian Beadwork

The finished size is 20 by 22 inches. A vast selection of beads is available wherever craft supplies are sold. They come in bulk or in small packages of one hundred or less. Purchase a small amount and test them for size on your canvas, then buy enough to finish the project plus a few extra.

Work up 2 or 3 square inches and check. Beads should fit easily on the mesh squares. Unlike yarn, they cannot be adjusted in tight-fitting areas. The smallest fraction in excess will show up eventually and make your work uneven. It is best to select beads that are smaller and to allow a hairline space between them.

Stretch canvas on a frame that is large enough to encompass the entire design plus a 2-inch border all around. It is important to have this space inside the frame or it will be impossible to work up to the margin. Fold remaining fabric over the frame and staple or nail it securely.

Victorian beadwork with needlework background. Courtesy Mrs. Ann Holzer.

1 **Opaque beads**
☑ 2 **Glass beads**

Examine the graph on page 18. The heavy black outlines and single dots indicate the placement of opaque beads, and the slanted lines, the placement of crystal-clear beads. The unmarked squares indicate background and should be worked first.

Work the background in cross-sitich (page 172). Use an even tension with all top stitches facing in the same direction. Simply count the squares in the unmarked areas of the graph and stitch back and forth across the canvas.

Do not carry tapestry yarn under areas designated for beads. This tends to create an undesirable padding that will give the beading uneven support.

When the background is completed, fill in the rest of the canvas with beads where indicated, first the opaque white and then the crystal clear. The beads in this work are fairly large and do not require a very fine needle. Try the darners, numbers 8 through 10, and use a strong thread specially designed for beadwork.

Wax thread lightly and double it for extra strength. Work beads as you would half cross-stitch, placing each bead on the cross-over point of the canvas. The threaded needle is pulled through to the right of the work, the bead is slipped over the needle, and the stitch is completed as the needle is brought back to the underside.

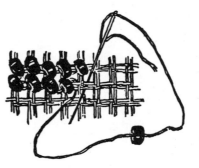

Work lines from left to right and reverse needle on the return row. Flip diagram of stitch detail to see position of needle. Use short strands of thread, and be sure to fasten them securely at the beginning and at the end.

Beads should be of the best quality and of an even size. Those made of glass are superior to plastic and will not turn cloudy or yellow.

Note: The original beadwork is stitched with dark blue tapestry yarn. Two-ply Persian-type or crewel yarn may be used instead. The cross-stitch requires a thinner thread than the half cross, so pretest yarn for coverage. The entire design may be worked in needlework in a combination of mat and polished threads.

Beadwork should be framed and never covered with glass.

Beading on Tulle   The type of beading shown in Plate 1 was used to trim elaborate dresses and gowns in the eighteenth and nineteenth centuries. The pattern may be duplicated easily from the color plate and then enlarged.

Draw or trace the design outline on a sheet of white paper and color in the areas as indicated. Use quick-drying marking pens.

Take a length of good-quality nylon tulle and pin it to the fabric. Fasten the tulle and the paper pattern to a frame large enough to accommodate the entire design, which should be clearly visible under the tulle.

Sort the beads in a muffin pan according to color and shape. Thread beading needle with thread to match tulle. Fasten at one end and work a running stitch through the tulle mesh following the design outline. Each time the needle comes to right side of work, thread a bead on it. The longer beads require longer stitches. Thread beads one at a time through the tulle but not through the paper. Follow design outline and color as indicated.

To repeat pattern, unpin paper and slide unworked tulle over design outline at an appropriate distance from finished portion. Line up design, pin in place, and continue working.

Note: Tulle beading lends itself to any simple hard-edge design and may be finished as an attractive window hanging.

AMERICAN NEEDLEWORK

The United States is the largest importer of needlecraft materials in the world. It is the proving ground for just about every kind of thread, fabric, and gadget. We have here, without doubt, the largest number of needlepoint retail shops and teaching establishments that dispense needlepoint information to the uninitiated (often by the uninitiated). Needlepoint, decorative needlework, creative stitchery, embroidery, or whatever you may call it, is a big leisure pastime in the United States and it is growing by leaps and bounds. We do, of course, have some very fine instructors; and although the schools have not yet been standardized, many are operated by professionals who employ competent and dedicated teachers.

There are also many organizations and clubs that operate on a national level. They charge a nominal fee for membership in return for which they send a number of mailings with information of interest to craftsmen about forthcoming exhibits, juried shows, lectures given by prominent professionals, and lists of instructors and suppliers.

Most of these organizations handle crafts in all media. Their yearly exhibits, such as the one sponsored by the New York Craftsman, are very interesting and should be attended by everyone who dabbles in creative arts and crafts.

The one active organization dedicated exclusively to the art of stitchery is the Embroiderers' Guild of America, with national headquarters in New York City and active chapters all over the country. The Guild offers very informative lectures, juried shows in which all members may participate, classes for beginners, and some of the best training courses for would-be teachers. A membership in the Embroiderers' Guild is a worthwhile investment for anyone interested in creative stitchery.

Contemporary needlework in America covers the whole spectrum of stitchery around the world. Antique needlework is protected with pride and affection and sometimes reproduced with a feeling of nostalgia, but the trend is toward the new, the bold, and the exciting.

On the next few pages are some examples of the versatility of American contemporary needlework. The one exception is the antique Log Cabin coverlet (page 41). It was introduced not only as a remembrance of things past but because ths pattern has been recently rediscovered and adapted to many forms of stitchery as well as crocheting and knitting.

Try your hand at some or all of these or top them with an original creation of your own.

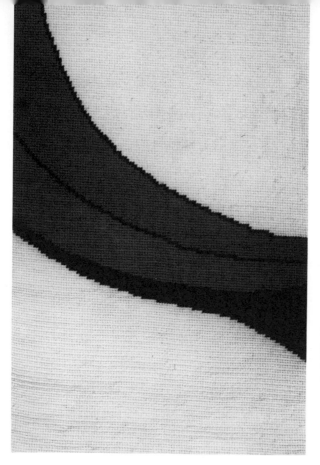

Contemporary needlepoint rug. Background: yellow (top and bottom). Stripes: medium green and magenta, separated by black lines. Designed and worked by the author.

The rug shown above was worked on number 5 mesh canvas with heavy Paternayan rug yarn. It may also be worked with three-ply Persian yarn. In order to cover the number 5 canvas adequately you need five full triple strands or fifteen-ply yarn. In any case, yarn should always be pretested for coverage before beginning a project.

INSTRUCTIONS

Materials

1½ yards of number 5 double-mesh canvas, 40 inches wide
½ pound of rug yarn in each of the center stripe colors
5 pounds of rug yarn for background
Tapestry needle to accommodate yarn and canvas

Heavy canvas should have a fold-back margin of at least 3 inches on the selvage and 6 inches on the cut edge. If 40-inch-wide canvas is not available, make the design smaller or use a different canvas gauge. This rug should not be worked in sections.

To begin, machine stitch cut edges of canvas and outline border. Enlarge design and transfer it to canvas (see general instructions, pages 8–11). This design may be drawn freehand directly on the canvas. Color lightly. There is no need to color the background.

Work in continental stitch from right to left and in half cross-stitch from left to right on return rows (see stitch details, page 175). This creates an interesting ribbed effect and is recommended only when it does not conflict with a complicated design. Alternate rows accurately and be sure to match direction of stitches in all the color changes so that the stripes are uniform.

Finish as a wall hanging, as a small area rug, or mount it on a frame. A canvas work of this size should be finished professionally.

Contemporary Rug II   The bright, informal, unshaded design of the rug in Plate 2 was adapted from a silk print. The design outline is simple enough to trace from the color plate. The actual size of this rug is 40 by 60 inches. Canvas mesh is number 4.

INSTRUCTIONS

Materials

2 yards of number 4 double-mesh rug canvas, 46 inches wide
1 pound each of Paternayan Persian or rug yarn in each of the following colors: bright pink, light pink, mint green, white, and gold
½ pound deep purple yarn
Largest tapestry needle
Felt marking pens in colors indicated

The canvas should have a fold-back margin of at least 3 inches on the selvage and 6 inches or more on the cut edge. If a 46-inch canvas is not available, make a smaller pattern or select canvas in a different gauge. This rug should not be worked in sections.

Enlarge design tracing to desired size. Machine stitch canvas along cut edges and outline border. Transfer design to canvas following general instructions on pages 9–11. Color lightly.

Work in basketweave stitch (page 176). You will need six full strands of three-ply Persian yarn (eighteen-ply). Cut skeins at one end only, count three strands, and fold in half after threading needle. Double rug yarn on number 4 canvas.

This rug design may be transferred to number 5 canvas and worked with single strands of rug yarn or five full strands of three-ply Persian yarn. It may also be worked on number 10 canvas with three-ply or standard tapestry yarn. (Remember, always pretest yarn for coverage before beginning a project.)

For best results, the rug should be finished professionally.

Contemporary Rug III   This rug design, Plate 3, was worked on number 10 single-mesh canvas with full three-ply Paternayan Persian yarn. The actual size is 36 by 58 inches.

INSTRUCTIONS

Materials

66 inches of number 10 single-mesh canvas, at least 40 inches wide
Yarn in the following quantities:
1½ pounds of dark green
½ pound each of light green and white
¼ pound each of dark turquoise, lavender, medium and dark purple, and medium red
2 ounces each of medium rust, light rust, and light turquoise
Tapestry needle, number 17

Machine stitch cut edges. Outline inside border to allow a 36-by-58-inch area for rug pattern. Enlarge the diagram opposite by photostat to the same dimensions and transfer it to canvas (see general directions on pages 9–11).

Color lightly as indicated on color plate and work in basketweave stitch (page 176). Continental stitch is not recommended for rugs unless they are worked on a frame.

Note: The design may be reduced or enlarged. Should it be made larger, it is important to obtain canvas wide enough to accommodate the entire rug, including a minimum border allowance of 2 inches all around. All rugs should be blocked and mounted professionally.

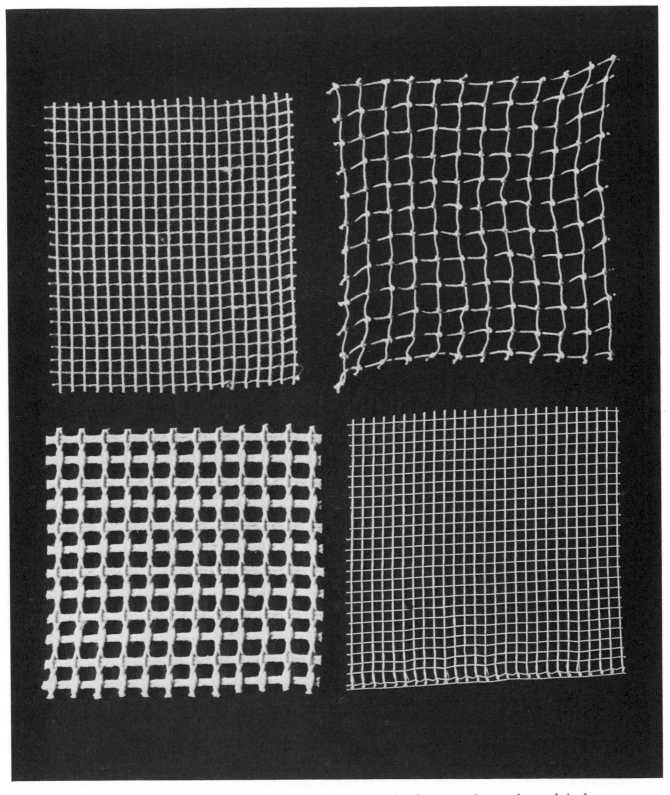

Upper left: number 6 netting; *upper right*: commercial fishnet number 4; *lower left*: leno canvas number 4; *lower right*: nylon Gardisette number 8.

Needleweaving on fishnet or filet lace was very popular at the turn of the century. It looked like lace and was used to make tablecloths, curtains, doilies, and lacy ornaments on blouses and lingerie.

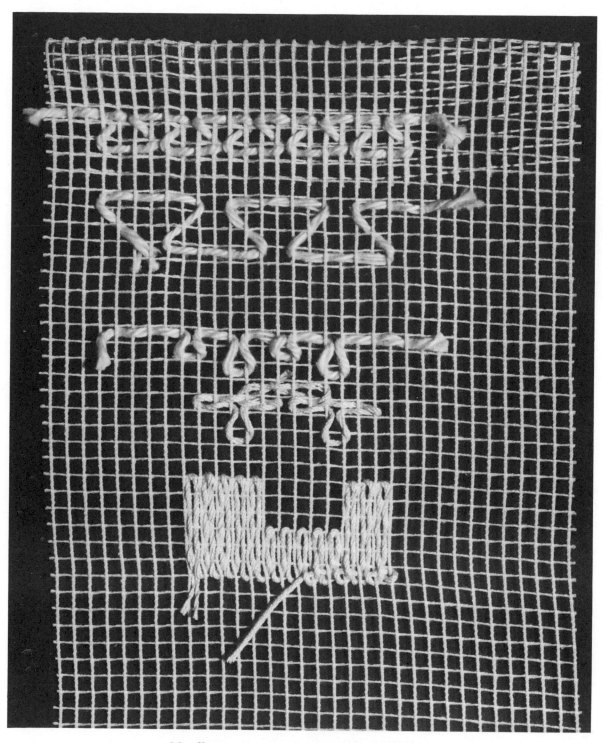

Needleweaving on soft, interlocked JES net.

Filet work on darning net. Patterns for doilies and a tablecloth or curtain. Samples courtesy JES Handicrafts.

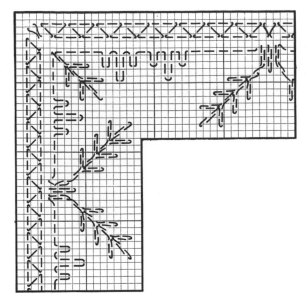

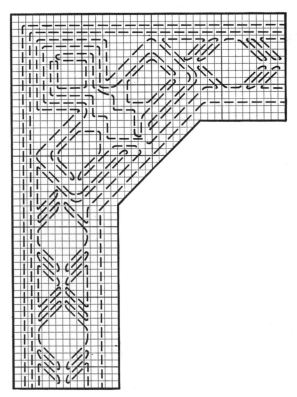

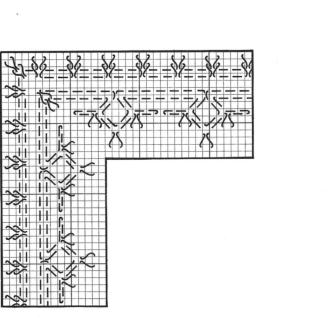

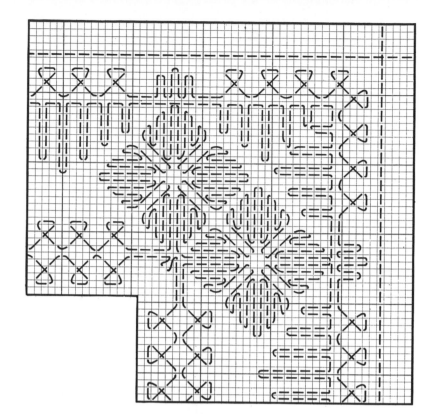

31

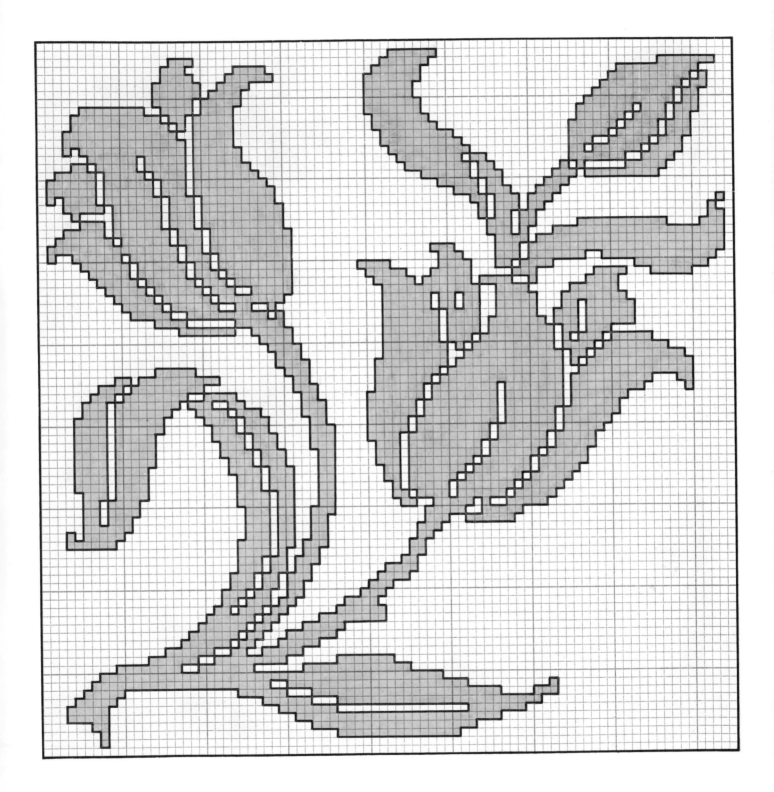

"Tulips." Needleweaving on number 4 mesh canvas. Worked by the author and shown in *Ladies' Home Journal Needle and Crafts*, Spring/Summer 1976. © Dow Communications.

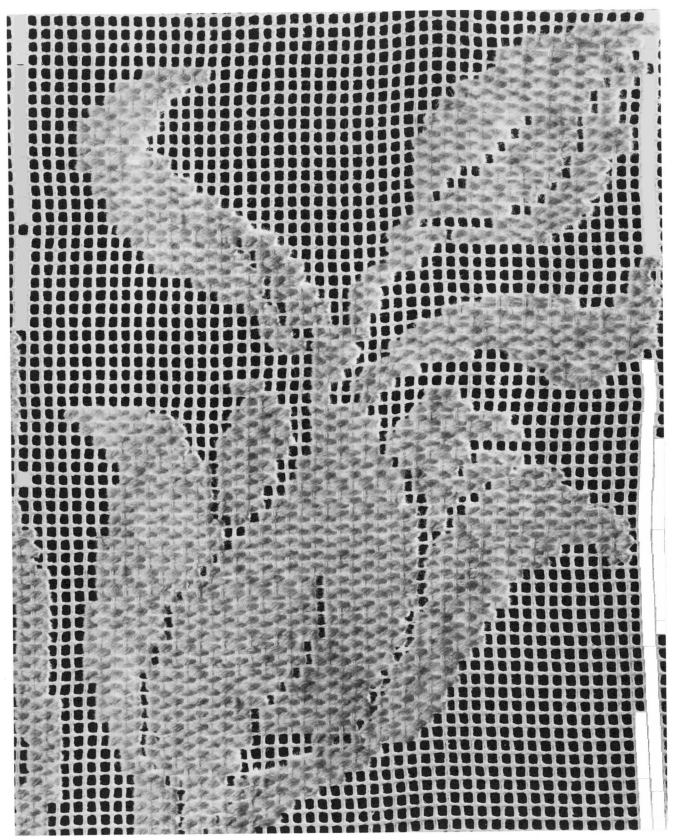

Detail of "Tulips."

"Tulips" is an adaptation of this technique. A heavy-gauge number 4 mesh canvas has the same grid as fishnet, but it is heavier and more rigid and therefore easier to handle. This pattern may also be worked on number 5 mesh or any gauge of locked-mesh fabric.

INSTRUCTIONS

Count the number of squares on the canvas mesh plus a margin of at least 3 inches all around. Fold back the canvas ½ inch all around and work a close buttonhole stitch (page 175) over the fold. This will give a finished border and will prevent the canvas from fraying as you work.

The yarn used on the number 4 canvas is knitting worsted doubled. Fold yarn in half and secure it to the canvas by slipping the needle through the fold and over one canvas thread (see stitch detail, page 173).

Weave threaded needle over and under the canvas strands. Count the mesh squares and work pattern in horizontal rows. On the return row, weave the needle in reverse (see detail, opposite). The yarn will fill the mesh squares with two rows. If the thread is thinner, you might need to work three or four rows within each line of mesh to fill it in.

The purpose of the mesh weaving is to fill in some of the canvas squares so that they create an opaque design. This is very effective as a window shade.

For finer canvas, test compatible thread. Designs may be borrowed from any counted cross-stitch pattern and may also be worked in color.

In traditional drawnwork the weft, or horizontal, threads are drawn from a given fabric and the warp, or vertical, threads are manipulated in various ways to create an open or lacy design on opaque cloth.

This is a modern interpretation of drawnwork. Only a warp is prepared and the manipulation, or needleweaving, is worked directly on it without the need of drawing and then replacing the weft.

INSTRUCTIONS

Build a strong frame from 2-by-4-inch strips of lumber in the size you want and drive a row of 1-inch nails with large heads ¼ inch apart at the top and bottom of the frame and 1 inch apart at the sides. Keep the nails in straight, even rows about 1 inch away from the frame opening.

Take a ball of ordinary butcher's string and build a warp between the top and bottom rows of nails. Tie the string around the first nail at top left-hand corner and guide it up and down, over and under the nail heads. Keep the string taut and don't loop it around the nails. Tie the string securely around the last nail at the bottom right-hand corner and clip.

Now, cut a length of string, thread it through a large tapestry needle, and work a simple needleweaving stitch across the warp. Keep the woven bars uneven. For a bulkier effect, work with two warp threads instead of one. Examine stitch detail, right.

Weave from left to right, and as the rows are completed, pass the string around the nails to the right and to the left of the frame. Do this every inch or

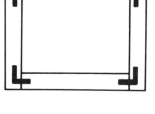

so as the nails line up with the finished rows. This will keep the work from pulling away from the frame.

Leave 2-inch tail ends at the beginning and at the end of each length of string and tie them together on the underside in a double knot. Don't clip ends too short. The knots will not become invisible but will stay in place on the underside of the work under the woven bars.

Butcher's string is not as flexible as tapestry yarn or embroidery thread, but it looks very striking in works where a coarser texture is desired.

The first and last tail end in the needleweaving should be folded back and stitched to the underside with ordinary sewing thread.

Remove all nails with pliers and slide two rods through the loops at top and bottom, or cut open the bottom row of loops and leave as fringe. The example

Needleweaving on string warp as seen in daylight. Design worked by the author.

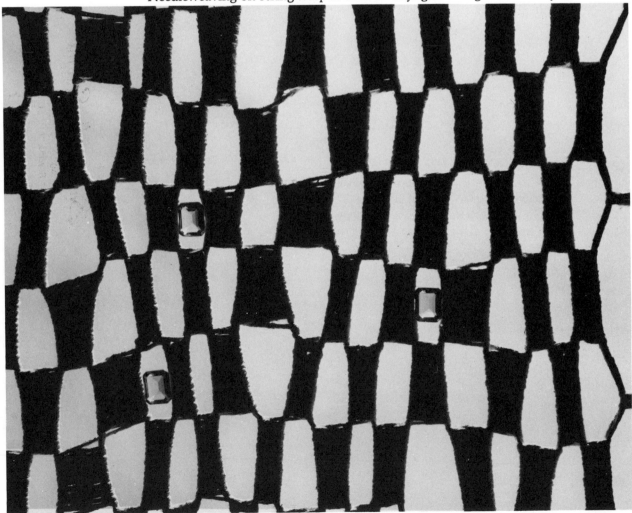

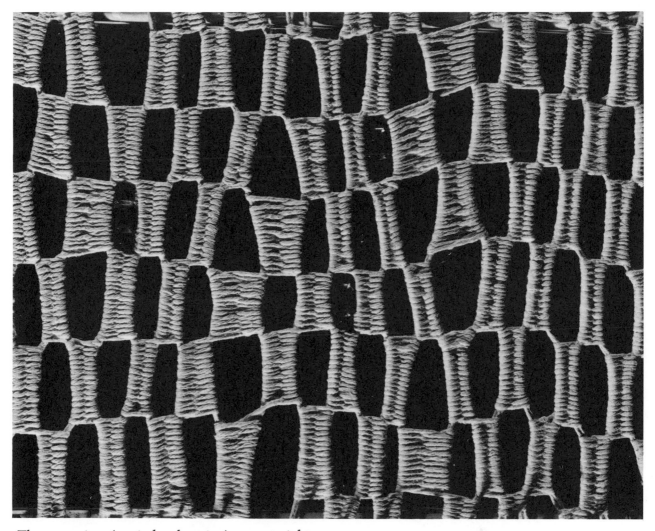

The same piece (a window hanging) seen at night.

shown here was framed inside a small window with several synthetic gemstones placed between stitches.

The photographs above and opposite show the same piece of string weaving in daylight and at night, with incandescent light accentuating the texture against the darkened window.

To make an attractive room divider, work the needleweaving directly on divider frames and finish by driving the nails flush with the wood. Cover nail heads with a thick crochet edging or wood strips and add hinges. Paint or stain frames before adding string.

Note: Other threads may be used in a project such as this: crochet thread in various gauges, linen warp, macramé cord, and a wide range of novelty strings—anything strong enough to withstand the pulling and twisting.

37

"Tropical Fish," Plate 4, is an excellent example of the flexibility of double-mesh canvas. Each design element is worked in a different stitch formation:

The fish in petit point, twenty stitches to the inch
The seaweed in gros point, or ten to the inch
Rock formations in bargello
The sandy floor in double cross-stitch in shaded outlines
The background in brick stitch

All stitches are compatible with the canvas and with each other. They compensate and do not overlap. Add to this a balanced design and a beautiful selection of colors, and you can see what happens to canvas stitchery in the hands of an artist.

INSTRUCTIONS

The actual size of the work is 30 by 30 inches. You will need one 36-inch square of double-mesh heavy-duty needlework canvas. The yarn estimate was not available but may be figured fairly accurately by allowing 1¼ yards per square inch of canvas for single stitches and double that for cross-stitches. Measure design segments at their widest and longest points and always buy a little more just to be sure.

Two tapestry needles are recommended: one for the petit point and one for the rest of the stitches.

Enlarge and transfer diagram following the general instructions on pages 8–11. Machine stitch cut edges and outline border all around.

Work fish, then plants. Follow with rock formation and sandy aquarium floor. Finish with background. Work colors as indicated in the color plate and stitches as described above. All yarns are Paternayan Persian. Stitch detail diagrams are shown on pages 172, 175, and below.

Bargello design for rock formation: work over six and under two strands of canvas and check color placement.

Bargello

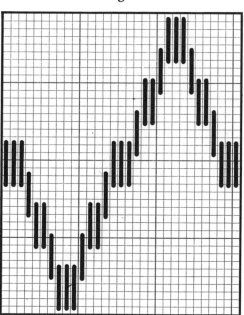

Brick stitch

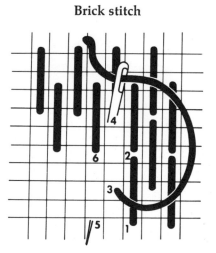

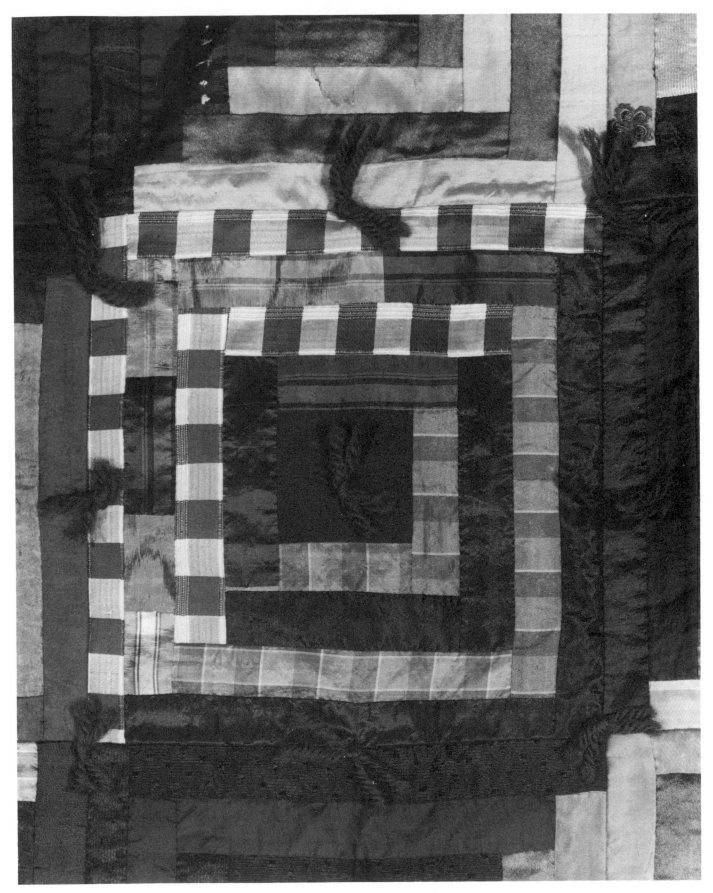

Detail of contemporary quilt, Log Cabin pattern.

The Log Cabin is one of the oldest and most popular of the American patch-work patterns. It may be assembled with the smallest pieces of fabric or ribbon of seemingly unrelated colors, reminiscent of crazy quilts.

Unlike the crazy quilt, the Log Cabin is constructed with geometric precision, as shown in Plate 5—an antique coverlet worked in the Deep Furrows pattern of the Log Cabin patchwork.

The basic principle of the Log Cabin patchwork is in the construction of a *unit square* with narrow strips of fabric "logs" cut in graduated sizes and positioned clockwise or counterclockwise around a center square. Each unit is assembled individually, and in the case of the Deep Furrows pattern, a diagonal color division line must be maintained at all times (see diagram on page 43).

When all the unit squares are completed, they are assembled into one large sheet, which is then lined and tufted. Traditionally, the Log Cabin patchwork is not quilted. It is used only as a decorative coverlet, as are most patchworks that require a great deal of intricate workmanship.

The Log Cabin pattern has long been a favorite with experienced quilters. The strips had to be cut and measured with great accuracy and stitched with small, nearly invisible stitches. It required a good eye for color and infinite patience. A fine patchwork in the Deep Furrows pattern was a sign of great expertise and a credit to the needleworker.

The actual size of the finished coverlet is 59 by 59 inches, including a 4-inch border, and it is made entirely of silk fabric.

INSTRUCTIONS

Materials

Enough scraps of silk fabric or ribbon to yield 1,600 strips (logs) 2½ to 5½ inches long and 2 inches wide, and 100 2-by-2-inch squares for centers (total 72 by 72 inches)

Dark silk fabric in small print or solid color for lining to measure 64 by 64 inches (may be assembled from two or more lengths)

Fine cotton fabric for interlining to measure 60 by 60 inches

Basting thread—a large spool in a bright, highly visible color

Sewing thread or six-strand embroidery floss in a neutral shade compatible with the fabrics

Heavy-gauge see-through plastic for pattern templates

Needle, scissors, pencil, ruler, and a large box of straight pins, plus a small magnet

Tufting thread or yarn

Silk fabric and ribbon are not difficult to obtain and may be purchased in small cuts in most fabric stores. If you decide to use scraps from old fabrics, select the ones that are clean and in good condition. Very old silk will not stand up well. Always cut strips on the straight of fabric. This is important to remember when working with bias-cut silk ties.

Divide shades into two categories: dark and light/bright. In general, navy, black, charcoal, and the darker values of wine, green, blue, or purple are considered dark shades. The rest are light/bright. Some light prints and plaids have a dark color that might be dominant in a small patch, and it is up to the individual to determine its category.

There are many ways to assemble a Log Cabin patchwork. In general, the small pieces of fabric (patches) are sewn together into a large sheet. The smaller the patches, the more time-consuming the work.

An easier way, although one that is not necessarily faster, is to work it in appliqué. Each unit is pinned and basted to a background square and may be repositioned instantly if need be. Patchwork is like a jigsaw puzzle, and I find it more manageable when assembled on a flat surface in appliqué.

This coverlet consists of one hundred 5½-by-5½-inch unit squares. The units are assembled individually and then pieced together in rows of ten. The rows are sewn together to form a square 55-by-55-inch sheet.

To begin, cut the interlining into one hundred 6-by-6-inch squares. Select a fine, compact cotton or cotton blend fabric that handles easily and is slow to ravel. These are the background squares.

Prepare the pattern templates. Heavy-gauge, semirigid plastic that can be cut with scissors is best, because a patterned fabric may be seen through it and adjusted to advantage before cutting. Plastic protective covers used in loose-leaf photography albums are excellent as templates. Cut them in 2-, 3-, 4-, and 5-inch lengths and all in ½-inch widths. Also cut one 1½-by-1½-inch square for centers. Cut an additional 5½-by-5½-inch template in heavy cardboard.

Begin by building one unit square. Each unit has sixteen strips of fabric and one center square. There are four strips in each dimension: two dark and two light/bright. The center is light/bright.

Select fabrics from the two categories and cut enough strips for one unit. Position the plastic template on a piece of fabric and outline it with a pencil or fine-line indelible marking pen. Cut the strip of fabric with an additional fold-back margin of ¼ inch all around.

Place the 5½-by-5½-inch cardboard template on a square of cotton interlining and draw an outline around it.

Miter (see photo opposite) and fold back the ¼-inch margin allowance on all fabric strips. Press to get a sharp crease and pin in place. *Follow construction technique in diagrams A to G opposite. Shaded areas indicate dark fabrics. Figure H indicates placement of unit squares.*

Baste with little stitches, remove pins, and set aside. With a little practice, you will be able to construct two or more units at the same time.

For best results, fabric strips should be straight and even and of the same general weight. They should line up closely to fit inside the 5½-by-5½-inch outline on the 6-by-6-inch square of interlining.

The remaining ½-inch border is needed for piecing the units into one coverlet.

Do not precut too many strips and do rotate the fabrics so that some of the more unusual patterns receive a fairly even distribution.

Wait until a large number of squares are basted before stitching them permanently to the background. This way you can alternate the business of building and basting new squares and going back to finish stitching older ones. Use small, nearly invisible stitches around each strip. Remove basting thread. (I might add that this is where you will realize the importance of bright, highly visible basting thread.)

When all the squares are completed (one hundred units), pin them to a wall in the Deep Furrows design assembly. This is a type of Log Cabin construction that shows dark and light diagonal stripes across the coverlet (see diagram H opposite).

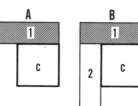

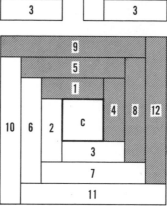

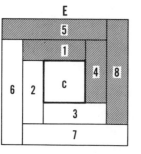

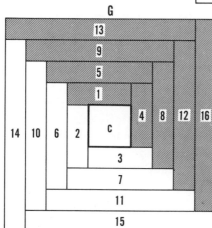

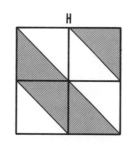

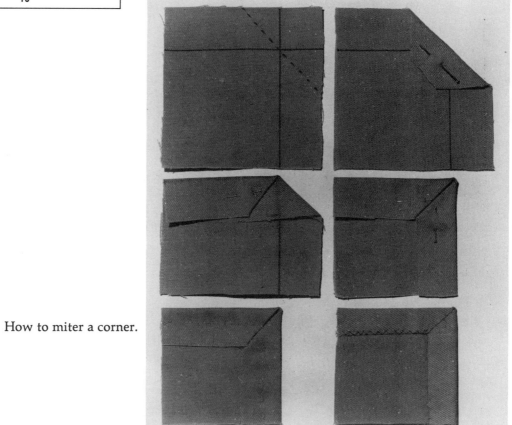

How to miter a corner.

Line up the squares ten across and ten down with dark sides against dark sides and light sides against light. Each square will have a diagonal division of dark and light and may be flipped either way.

Fold back the margin allowance as you pin the squares and step back to survey the total effect. The stripes are more pronounced at a distance and a Deep Furrows coverlet makes a striking wall hanging in a large room.

Unpin one row of squares at a time and stitch them together along the ¼-inch margins. Press seams to one side. Stitch the ten rows to one another and your coverlet top is completed. Before lining, check to make sure that the white margins are thoroughly hidden on the underside and are not visible between the appliqué units. Clip all loose threads and any visible bits of basting. Press the entire work on the wrong side.

To line, assemble lining fabric into a 64-by-64-inch square. Place lining wrong side up on a large, flat surface such as an uncarpeted floor. Position the finished coverlet top in the center and measure the border carefully. It should extend exactly 9 inches all around.

Place some heavy books in the center and smooth fabric with your hands until it relaxes and lies perfectly flat. Run some large basting stitches in rows at 2-inch intervals across the length and width of the coverlet and tuft it.

Tufting is a stitch technique used in layered needlework to prevent the fabrics from shifting or ballooning. It is faster than quilting and is often used on quilts and coverlets with elaborate designs where quilting patterns may prove competitive. Use a strong thread or yarn in a compatible shade and a sharp-pointed needle. Bring threaded needle through all layers of fabric and bring it back one small stitch away. Cut thread, leaving 2 inches at both ends, to be tied in a double knot.

Tuft the Log Cabin coverlet at all points where the four corners of four square units meet and also in the center squares. The tufts may be left on the right side or on the wrong side of the coverlet.

Once tufting is completed, place coverlet on a large, flat surface and recheck margins. Miter corners and fold lining over the edges of coverlet. Allow 1-inch fold-back on lining fabric over the remaining ½ inch of interlining that extends from the stitched squares. Pin borders from center point to the right and left toward the corners.

Borders should be straight and even. Baste carefully and remove pins. Finish with close herringbone stitches all around and into miters. Remove all basting threads and clip all loose threads.

Tufting and finishing may be done on a table surface without a frame once the fabrics are properly basted.

Note: The Log Cabin pattern may be varied in a number of ways. The unit squares may be enlarged or reduced by increasing or diminishing the number or size of fabric strips.

Photograph Quilt   This is a new approach to a very old needlework technique. A photograph is enlarged to king-size proportions, separated into component parts that are then traced on fabric, cut out, worked in a giant appliqué, and quilted. The result is quite startling and the idea is original.

Materials

Satin background in desired dimensions
Fabric for lining in the same size
Quilt batting in the same size (polyester is preferable)
Assorted fine fabrics for appliqué (satin, brocade, etc.)
Quilting and embroidery threads
Appropriate needles
Bright basting thread
Tracing paper
Indelible marking pen with fine point
Pencil, pins, scissors, small brush, and Elmer's glue
Photograph of your choice

The first step is to find a photograph you like. The best is one that is animated: a funny face, a smile, a wink, or any expression characteristic of a particular individual. Select a high-contrast photograph with clearly visible outlines.

Next, have a photostat made to the actual size of your projected work. This is essential for best results.

You will need a large work area. Place a sheet of tracing paper over the photostat (tape several sheets together if necessary) and pin in place. Trace the entire outline of the photostat as well as any parts of the picture that are *not* going to to be cut out in appliqué. Make a second tracing, and this time outline all the parts that *will* be cut out in appliqué: hair, hat, collar, lapels, eyebrows, and so on. Number all parts and indicate these numbers in the corresponding areas on the photostat for cross-reference. Tack both photostat and photograph near your work area.

Press all fabrics. Satins, velvets, brocades, and similar fine fabrics are most popular for this type of quilt.

Place background fabric on a large, flat surface and fasten with push pins to prevent shifting.

Position *first* tracing on background as it looks in the photostat and slide carbon paper in between. Pin in several places and transfer the entire *outline*.

Select appropriate fabrics for appliqué pieces. Cut out the numbered sections from the *second* tracing and use them as paper patterns.

Turn the paper patterns wrong side up and pin them to the wrong side of the fabrics. Outline patterns with bright indelible markers.

Brush the outlines with some diluted Elmer's glue (equal parts water and glue) and let dry. This prevents the fabric from fraying when cut. Cut out all pattern pieces. If there is a large number of similar fabric cutouts, number them as you did the second paper tracing.

When the cut pattern sections are turned right side up, they will face in the right direction and fit inside the main outline.

Pin the sections in their proper position as if assembling a large puzzle. It is not necessary to fold back the margins of the cut fabrics. The glue will prevent fraying, and this way you will achieve a clearer, sharper "photographic" image.

Baste securely with bright, highly visible thread and remove pins.

The next step is very important. It serves to outline details that are not worked in appliqué but are essential to the final picture. Position the *first* paper tracing over the appliqué work, line up outlines, and pin in place.

Machine stitch all facial features, lines, and wrinkles right through the paper

Photograph quilt. Designed and worked by Karen Katz, courtesy Sewn Arts.

with neutral-colored thread and wide-gauge stitches. Remove pins and peel off paper. Transfer or carbon paper does not work well on velvets and brocades, and the machine stitching will be covered with embroidery.

Hang appliqué on the wall near the original photograph and step back to see if the resemblance is there. Adjust if necessary.

Stitch appliqué pieces around outlines with small running stitches in threads to match fabrics and remove bastings.

Place appliqué work over a sheet of polyester batting and a lining of your choice under that. Baste the three layers together and fasten to a quilting frame. Embroider appliqué outlines and various features through the three layers of fabric. Work stitches in two motions as in all quilting. Some outlines may be worked in chain or outline stitch. Others may require such heavier, bolder stitches as blanket, buttonhole, or herringbone. Much depends on the photograph and your interpretation of it.

Hang up the quilt periodically and step back to examine it. Add extra stitches here and there as needed. Don't expect a photographic likeness; all you need is a resemblance.

Quilt the background with small running stitches in matching or contrasting colors. Let the photograph quilt hang for several days before deciding that it is finished. Double-check small details such as loose threads, leftover bastings, and unfinished embroidery. All cut edges should be covered with stitches.

Finish quilt by folding in top and lining against each other. Trim any batting that shows and slip stitch all around. Add a binding that resembles a frame.

Note: The quilting and embroidery may be worked in whole or in part on a sewing machine with embroidery attachments.

Quilt from Artist's Pen-and-Ink Drawing

A pen-and-ink drawing achieves a new dimension when it is translated into a quilt (the term *quilting* refers to a type of padded stitchery, not necessarily the size of a bed cover).

The drawing is sketched or enlarged from a sketch with a fine-point acrylic pen on a sheet of drip-dry white fabric and placed over a layer of polyester batting with a lining under that. All three layers must be of equal size. The piece should be worked on a quilting frame.

INSTRUCTIONS

Use two strands of the six-strand embroidery floss in black or navy and work with small backstitches (not quilting stitches). Work through all three layers following design outline as precisely as possible.

If the border is wider than 3 inches, quilt one or two rows of running stitches at 1-inch intervals all around.

Remove quilt from frame and finish by folding back the edges against each other and working a tight overcast stitch all around. Place on a bed or hang on a wall. It is completely washable.

A quilt such as this may be worked in "negative." Transfer or sketch design on dark fabric (black, navy, brown, etc.) with white pencil and embroider with white thread.

See pages 8–11 for additional information on enlarging and transferring designs.

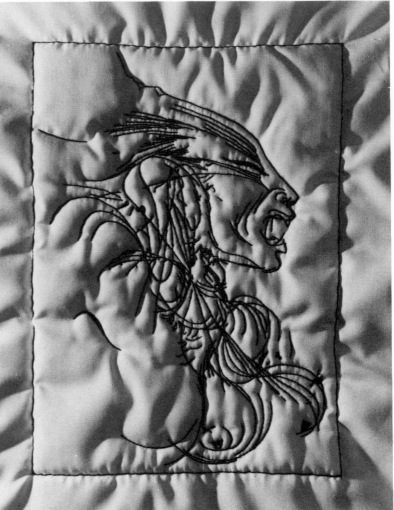

Trapunto quilt adapted from artist's sketch. Worked by the author.

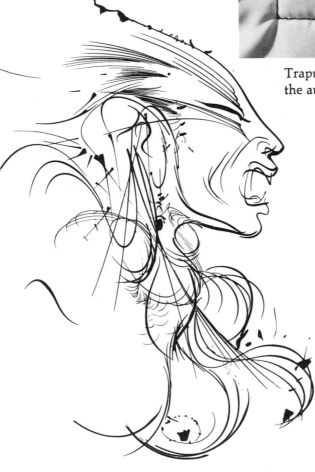

A chapter on American needlework would not be complete without at least one bargello design.

Bargello is based on a vertical stitch formation. It offers great flexibility in pattern construction and is one of the most popular forms of needlepoint in the United States at this time.

The zebra head inside a framework of black and white stripes (Plate 6) is one of the most elegant and truly original of the contemporary bargello designs.

INSTRUCTIONS

Materials

17-by-20-inch number 14 single-mesh canvas (includes border)
3 ounces each of black and white tapestry yarn
2 ounces of yarn for background—magenta or any other color
Number 17 tapestry needle

Work with two plies of three-ply Persian-type tapestry yarn. Tape or stitch canvas all around. Outline a 2-inch border, leaving a needlepoint surface 15 by 18 inches.

Begin at top center, twenty-six canvas strands below the border line, and work the first quarter of the lead line in white yarn. This is the first inner circle line. Work from center to the right as indicated in graph outline, page 50. Repeat in mirror image from center to left. Now work the entire lower half to complete the inner frame. Check to make sure that top and bottom center points correspond.

The zebra head is shown in a counted-stitch graph on page 51. The graph paper is ten squares to the inch and appears larger than needlework that is on fourteen-mesh canvas. Center head inside bargello framework with an approximate space of 1¾ inches from the top center and 1½ inches from the bottom center point. Work black stitches first, then white, and fill in with background.

For minimum distortion, work in basketweave stitch or use a frame for this part of your needlework. Bad distortion inside a bargello framework makes a piece very difficult to block. If you do sustain distortion, however, block the piece before you finish the bargello.

Once the center is completed, continue working the black and white from the center outward, alternating two rows in each shade except the inside row, which is single in white. Check Plate 6 for accuracy.

This is not a four-way bargello; it is worked in one direction. A framework such as this may be adapted to any center motif or around a photograph or mirror.

Note: Occasionally black wool tapestry yarn will shed dark filaments over a light adjacent color and make it appear soiled. If you encounter this, use black six-strand cotton embroidery floss (D.M.C. or Coats & Clark). The full six-thread strand will cover number 14 mesh canvas and will give a sharp, clean outline.

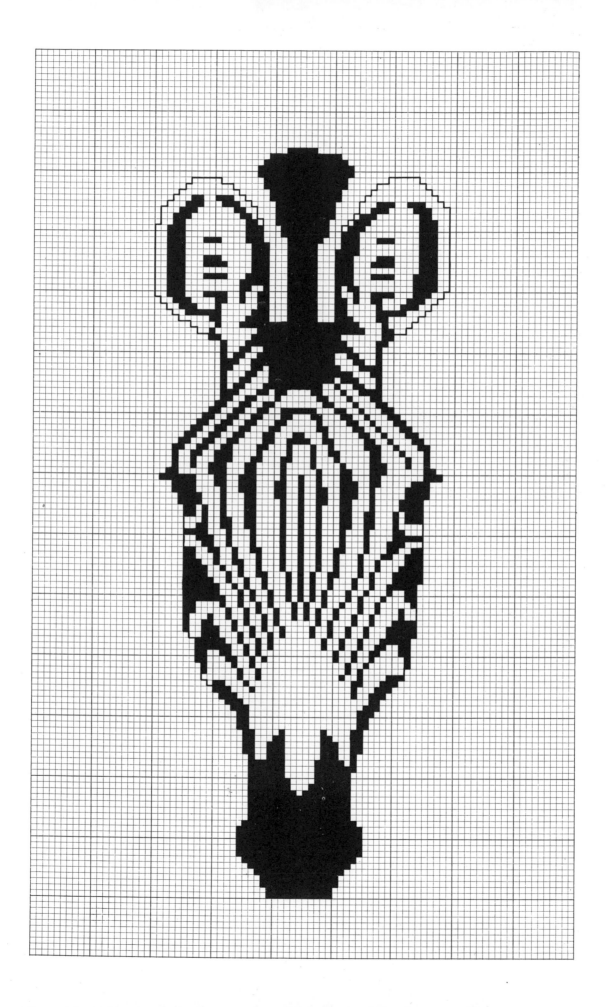

Crewel designs from English bed curtains. Victoria & Albert Museum.

Plate 1. Victorian beadwork on tulle. Courtesy Ann Holzer.

Plate 2. Contemporary needlepoint rug. Designed and worked by the author.

Plate 3. Contemporary needlepoint rug. Design adaptation by the author. Worked by Joan Hyman.

Plate 4. "Tropical Fish." Canvas needlepoint designed and worked by Roberta Frauwirth. Second-prize winner, professional category, 1975 Embroiderers' Guild Exhibit.

Plate 5. Antique patchwork coverlet, Log Cabin pattern. Courtesy Frieda Wenger Assoc.

Plate 6. Bargello with zebra head. Design courtesy Suzy Girard.

Plate 7. Painted canvas. Courtesy the Royal School of Needlework, London.

Plate 8. Painted canvas. Courtesy the Royal School of Needlework, London.

Plate 9. Embroidery based on a Celtic design, Ireland.

Plate 10. Fabric collage designed and worked by Kristina Friberg.

Plate 11. Swedish jacket and accessories.

Plate 12. Skirt bags.

Plate 13. Gloves and skirt bags.

All courtesy Nordiska Museum, Stockholm.

Plate 14. Embroidered dolls.
Variations on one pattern. Sweden.

Plate 15. "My Horse." Designed by Mirja Tissari and worked by the Friends of Finnish Handicraft.

Plate 16. Needlepainting from Holland. Silk on satin, signed W. Haelwech, 1650. Photo courtesy The Rijksmuseum, Amsterdam.

b

c

a

Plate 17. Embroidered tablecloth
from Kalocsa, Hungary.

Plate 18a, b, c. Details.

Plate 19. Embroidery on machine-made lace, Kalocsa, Hungary.

Plate 20. Matyo embroidered vest. Hungary.

Plate 21. Matyo embroidered pillowcase. Hungary. Courtesy of Roberta Frauwirth.

Plate 22. Rumanian national costume.
Courtesy of Mrs. Annette Peretz.

Plate 23. Detail of sleeve, showing beadwork.

Plate 24. Details of Bessarabian shirts, Rumania, and Hungarian embroideries.

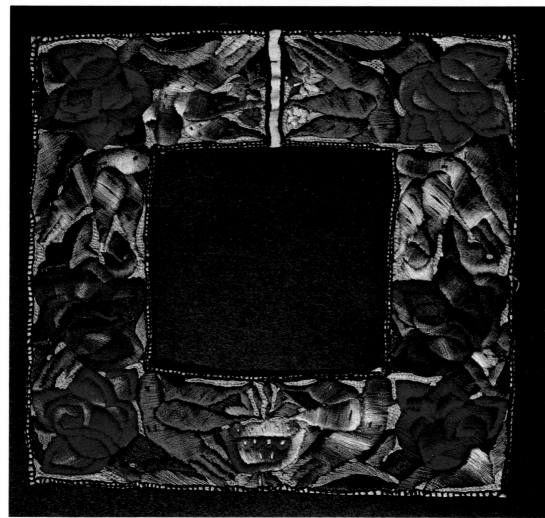

Plate 25. *Huipil* neckline worked in variegated threads. Quetzaltenango, Guatemala. Courtesy of Mr. Copeland H. Marks.

Plate 26. Detail of altar cloth, San Mateo Ixtatan, Guatemala. Author's collection.

Plate 27. "Glele"—the Lion—appliqué, Dahomey. Author's collection.

Plate 28. "Exodus." Felt appliqué wall hanging designed and worked by Kopel Gurwin, Israel. Courtesy the America-Israel Cultural Foundation, New York.

Plate 29. Bedouin dress made by Moslem Arabs. Author's collection.

Plate 30. *Camis* (kaftan), eighteenth-century India. The Metropolitan Museum of Art, Gift of Mr. and Mrs. Clarence S. Stein, 1962.

Plate 31. Chain stitch rug, Kashmir, India. Author's collection.

Plate 32. Burmese wall hanging (Kalaga), eighteenth century. Courtesy Mrs. Jean Wardell.

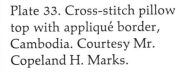
Plate 33. Cross-stitch pillow top with appliqué border, Cambodia. Courtesy Mr. Copeland H. Marks.

Plate 34. Enlarged detail of pillow top.

Plate 35. Chinese wall hanging, nineteenth century. Courtesy Mrs. Jean Wardell.

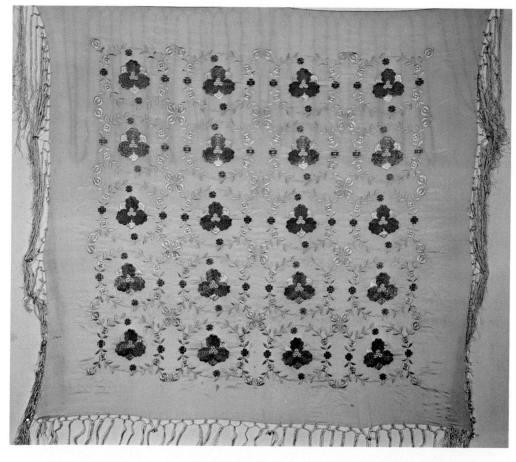

Plate 37. Shawl, late nineteenth or early twentieth century, China. Author's collection.

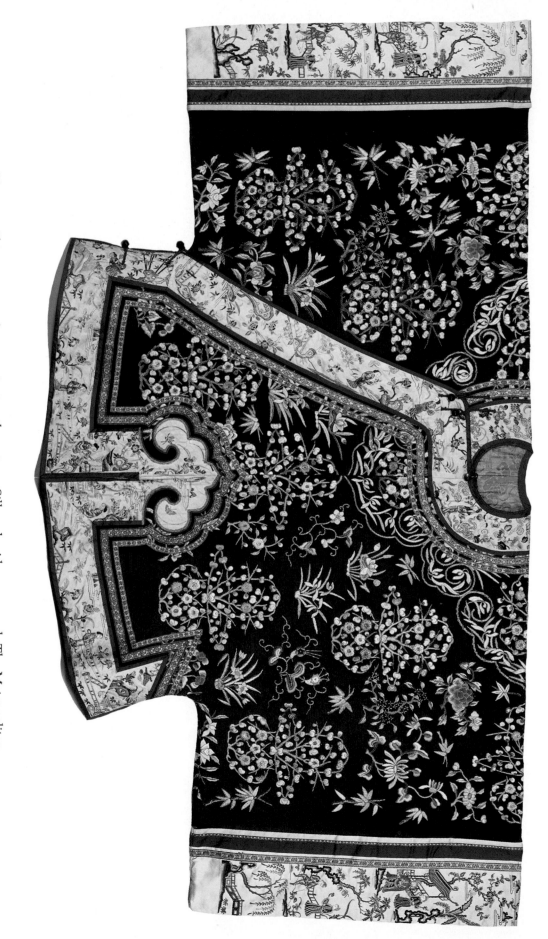

Plate 36. Chinese woman's coat, nineteenth century. Silk embroidery on wool. The Metropolitan Museum of Art. Dorothy A. Gordon and Virginia A. White in memory of Madge Ashley, 1973.

Plate 38. Shawl, early twentieth century, China. As seen in *Ladies' Home Journal Needle and Crafts.* Fall/Winter 1976. © Dow Communications. Author's collection.

Plate 39. Antique shawl, Italy. Author's collection.

Plate 40. Two *obi*, nineteenth century, Japan. "Cranes"—Tsuru—design, and "Fans"—Sensu—design. Courtesy Mrs. Jean Wardell.

Plate 41. Kimono. From the Kanebo Collection. Courtesy Kanebo Ltd., Osaka.

Plate 42. Kimono. From the Kanebo Collection. Courtesy Kanebo Ltd., Osaka.

ENGLISH NEEDLEWORK

English needlework has a long and proud history, and the collections on exhibit at the various British museums are some of the most spectacular in the world.

The English schools of needlework are excellent, and both teachers and students take their work seriously. The best known is the Royal School of Needlework in London under the patronage of H.M. Queen Elizabeth the Queen Mother. The school receives students from all over the world and is the best place to buy authentic old English designs for canvas stitchery. For additional information, see the list of suppliers, page 178.

I have selected four samples of needlework from England. Two from the Victoria and Albert Museum, fragments of seventeenth-century bed curtains, were chosen for their graceful simplicity and extra-large pattern repeat.

If you ever have the need for such patterns, they are easy to trace right from the black-and-white photographs and enlarge to any size. The one opposite (top) has a pattern repeat of 18 inches, and the other has a repeat of nearly 25 inches.

Both are worked in shades of green wool yarn on a cream-colored linen-wool blend fabric. The stitches are back, stem, running, chain, speckling, and various blanket and buttonhole stitch formations. The filled areas are worked with rows of stem stitches.

The designs may be interpreted in any combination of outline stitches and are excellent for bedspreads, curtains, or wherever a really large repeat is required.

The other two samples are from the Royal School of Needlework. These are reproductions of medieval designs for canvas stitchery and are an excellent choice for seat covers, footstools, pillows, or small framed pictures. They may also be enlarged to rug size.

These two designs (Plates 7 and 8) are shown in color on unworked canvas so that they would be easier to reproduce once the diagrams on pages 54 and 55 are traced. See the general directions on enlarging and tracing designs on canvas, pages 8–11.

IRISH NEEDLEWORK

In the early pre-Christian era, Ireland was part of a Celtic world that stretched from the Iberian Peninsula to the Scandinavian countries and from Hungary to the Atlantic coast of western Ireland. The Celtic people were far-flung, and communication between was slow and difficult. Yet the language, myth, ritual belief, and art were one.

They produced designs of true originality and style, which had a major influence on Irish art that can be traced back to the Bronze Age. There prevails a complex pattern of loops and spirals, triangles and squares. The lines flow into one another and the shapes adapt perfectly to stone engravings, metalwork, jewelry, and illuminated manuscripts. *The Book of Kells* is one of the most magnificent examples of the art of illumination—worth a trip to Trinity College in Dublin.

There are no samples of Celtic needlework, nor is there any indication of its having existed. But the Celtic element is still a guiding influence in Irish contemporary art, and needlework designs of Celtic origin are very popular.

Several design outlines suitable for blouse tops, borders, pillows, or any decorative objects are shown here. Enlarge them to a suitable size and trace them on iron-on patterns. They may be outlined in chain stitch (page 171), as in Plate 9, or in stem stitch (page 170), or they may be filled in with those stitches and outlined in gold thread or beads.

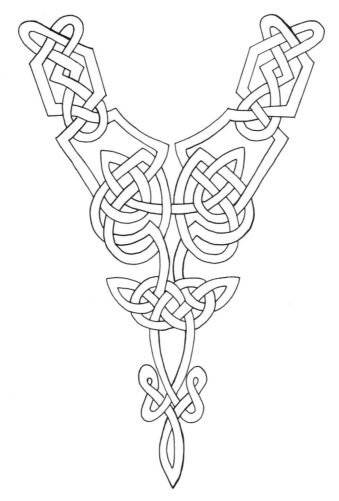

Carrickmacross Lace

There is ample evidence to show that lacemaking was in existence in the eighteenth century in Ireland and was taught at a school founded by the Dublin Society from 1731 to 1774.

Irish lace was reintroduced in the early part of the nineteenth century; but it wasn't until 1846, the year of the great famine, that it became a people's industry. Many lace schools were opened in various parts of the country as a relief measure, and they became a real source of income.

There are three distinct types of Irish lace: Limerick, Irish needlepoint or Youghal lace, and Carrickmacross. Irish needlepoint and Limerick lace have been adapted to machines and at this time are no longer being made by hand.

I was enchanted with the soft, airy quality of Carrickmacross lace when I visited Ireland. Although not a true lace and bearing a close resemblance to shadow appliqué, it is, nevertheless, called lace and is one of the few kinds still made entirely by hand.

The making of Carrickmacross appliqué is a small cottage industry operated by nuns at the Convent of St. Louis in Carrickmacross, County Monaghan, a five-hour bus ride from Dublin. The girls and women in the village learn this lovely craft at the convent and, once they become experienced, they receive work assignments to execute at home, or the "cottage." The convent acts as the control center. This is very important in a cottage industry. It is a way of maintaining quality in workmanship, of providing a uniform training program, and of establishing prices so that the women receive a decent wage for their work. Also, materials may be purchased in quantity and therefore more economically. The convent handles all sales distribution. Carrickmacross lace items such as handkerchiefs, collars and cuffs, mantillas, and especially communion and wedding veils are favored in boutique shops around the world.

Small Prayer Shawl

INSTRUCTIONS

Materials

½ yard of white tulle or bridal veiling
½ yard of white organdy (drip-dry)
Two skeins of very fine white perle cotton thread*
Two skeins of white six-strand cotton embroidery floss
One sheet of tracing paper, medium weight, 20 by 24 inches
Black fine-line *indelible* marker
Sharp-pointed embroidery scissors
Thimble and sharp embroidery needles to accommodate threads

The actual size of the shawl is 18 by 22 inches.

The pattern diagrams are illustrated on pages 60–62 (one square = one inch). Fold tracing paper in half lengthwise and run thumbnail along fold.

Trace both top and bottom parts of diagram (pages 60 and 61) on folded tracing paper, aligning dotted center line very accurately with the fold. Turn paper over and trace second half of diagram from your first tracing, which should be clearly visible. Unfold paper and you have the complete design.

*The threads recommended in this chapter are not the same as those used at St. Louis Convent but are the nearest I could match from readily available sources.

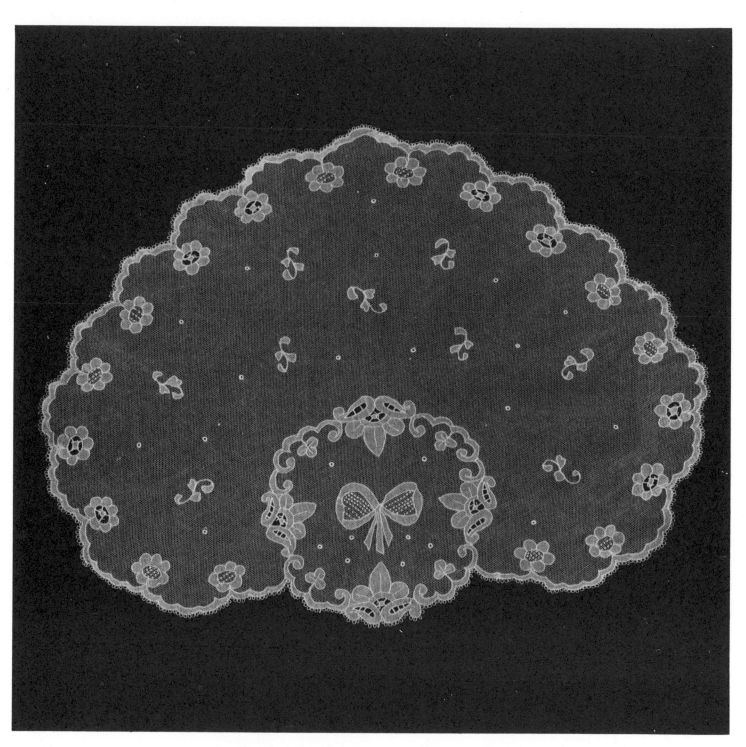

Small veil of Carrickmacross lace. Author's collection.

Top

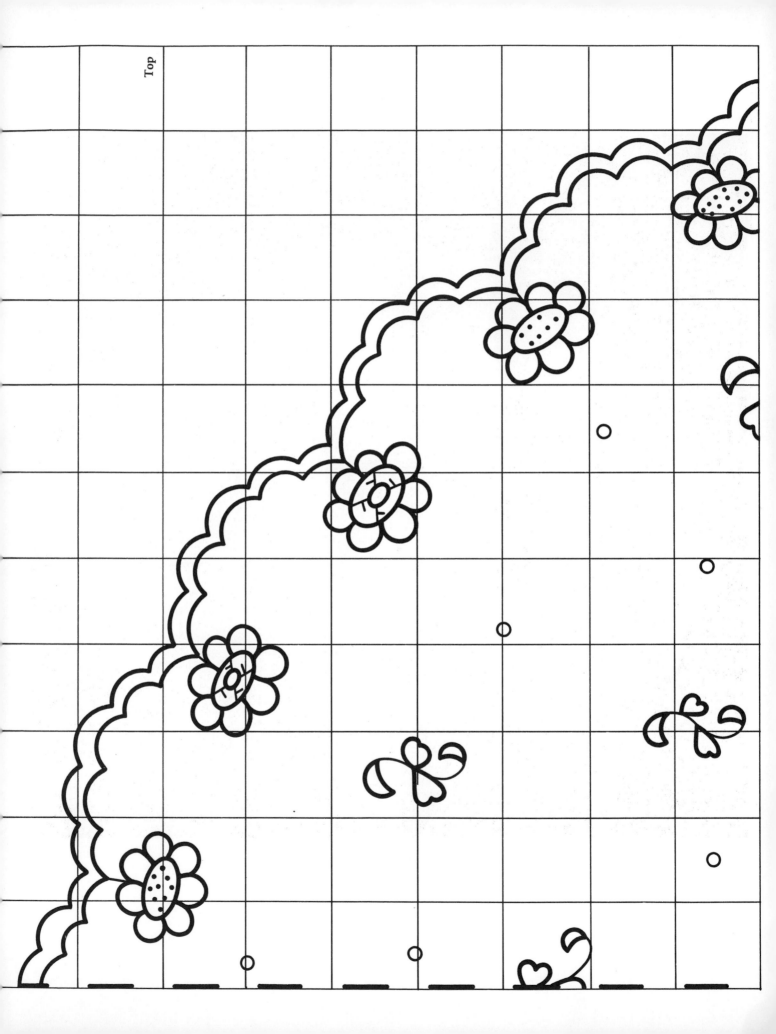

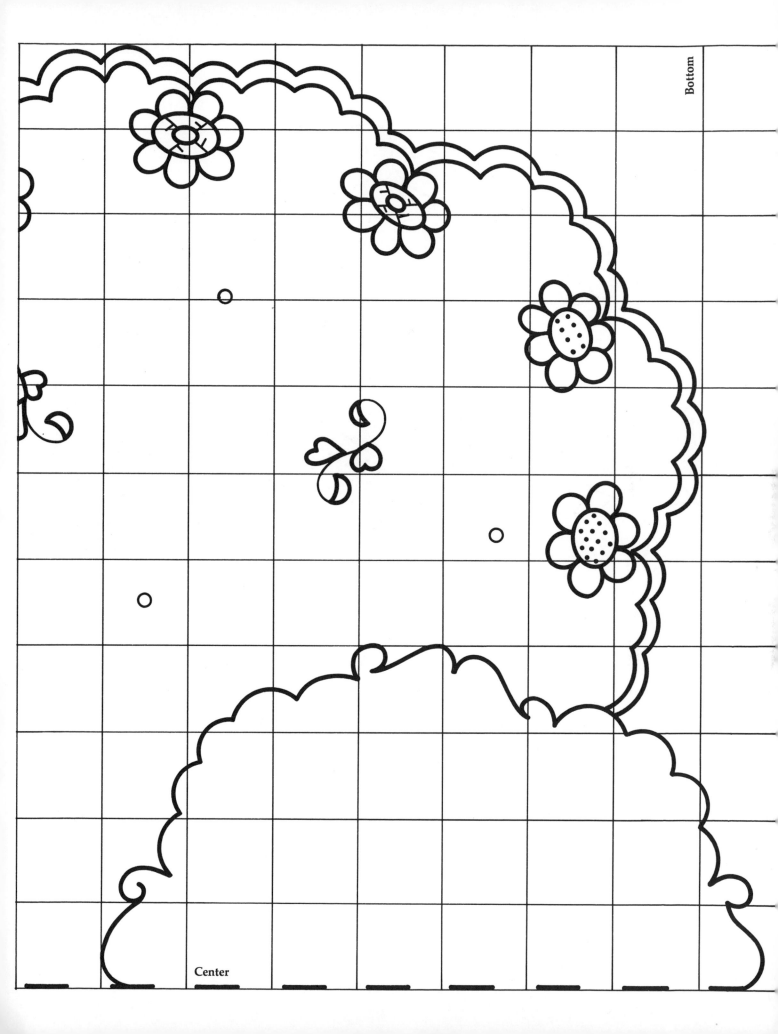

Bottom

Center

Medallion center is shown opposite. Position tracing-paper pattern over medallion so that it fits into the center outline and trace. This is your pattern. Enlarge it according to the directions on pages 8–9.

All tracing should be done with a highly visible black pen or marker. It should be absolutely indelible or it will come off on your white fabric as you work.

Place tulle over paper pattern and organdy over tulle and baste the three layers with colored basting thread. Basting threads should be visible so that they may be removed easily.

The experienced Carrickmacross worker pins the layers together, but I find basting more reliable. Baste horizontal lines at 1-inch intervals across the entire surface of the three layers of paper and fabric. Tulle and organdy are rather slippery, and basting will keep them in place.

Carrickmacross lace is worked with a simple couching outline stitch. Pattern outline should be clearly visible through both fabrics. Follow it with the perle cotton thread and overcast with small couching stitches worked fairly close, using single strands of the six-strand embroidery floss. Fasten and trim tail ends carefully.

Work this couching embroidery through the three layers. Traditionally, this is worked in the hand; but if you prefer, you may fasten the work on a frame. However, the frame must be large enough to accommodate the entire pattern. Do not use an embroidery hoop. It will crush your paper and mar the design outline.

When all outlines are couched, gently peel away the paper pattern, which will be held down only with tiny stitches and may be used again. Cut away the organdy close to the couching outline (it will not fall apart). Be careful not to nick the tulle. The flower and ribbon centers are filled in with guipure or darning stitches (see photo, page 64) that are designed to conform with the hexagon shape of tulle net formation. The guipure stitches are shown on pages 64 and 65 and should be practiced first on chicken-wire mesh, which is also a hexagon.

The border is worked in couching outline, cut close, and finished with an edging of picot. This is a looped thread of perle cotton fastened to the border with tiny stitches in single-strand embroidery floss (see stitch detail, page 172).

Picot edging for Carrickmacross lace. Work from left to right. Loop a strand of perle cotton along the edge of finished lace article. Thread a needle with a finer thread, such as two strands of six-strand embroidery floss, and place two small stitches inside each loop. For best results, the perle cotton should be in one continuous filament. If you must attach new thread, tie it with a weaver's knot and place it inside the loop under the stitches.

64

Carrickmacross lace fills worked on tulle. These are two stitches used to fill the larger open areas on the Carrickmacross veils: *a* is worked inside geometric spaces and *b* is worked at random and is very effective on an otherwise plain expanse of tulle background. Both stitch diagrams are very explicit and need no additional description.

a

b

Weaver's knot. When working on open mesh such as filet lace or tulle, finishing tail ends may cause unsightly bulges. To avoid this, tie the end of the old thread to the new one with a weaver's knot, as follows: Allow about 3 inches of thread at both ends. Begin by tying one thread end into a conventional knot but don't pull the end out. Instead, pull it out into a loop and slip the new thread end into it. Close the knot until the new thread slides into the loop with a little click. Tighten the knot by pulling at opposite ends of the threads (upper right and lower left and reverse). If properly made this knot will not pull out even when the ends are clipped short. Practice this with threads in two different colors.

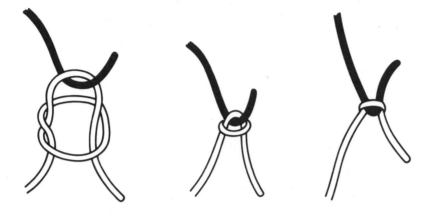

Point de toile. Translated, it means "cloth stitch." Anchor the thread with a small knot in the corner of your mesh or, if doubled, use the slip knot. Weave the thread over and under the mesh both horizontally and vertically. Examine the stitch detail carefully. The lines of the threads are fairly open for easy identification but in reality they should fill the mesh like cloth. The heavier the threads, the more textured your filet. Heavy threads may be woven once or twice through the mesh rather than three times. It is possible to weave filet in one direction only. This is called *point de reprise* and it requires extra-heavy yarn to fill the mesh. It is also easier to work.

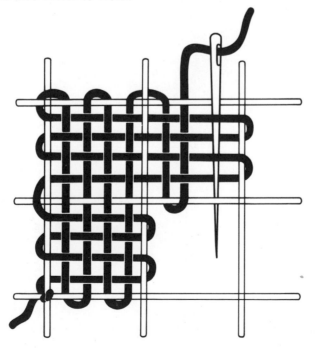

Carrickmacross collar and cuffs set. Author's collection.

Additional examples of Carrickmacross lace are shown opposite and below. The lovely collar and cuffs set may be easily reproduced from the photograph. Practice on a small piece first. Once you gain experience, work on a larger piece, such as the heirloom bridal veil, the designs for which are shown on page 68.

Note: Although original Carrickmacross lace is worked in couching outline, I don't see why it cannot be worked in buttonhole stitch instead. It would make a slightly coarser outline, but it would not require two separate threads as in couching. You might use two strands of the six-strand embroidery floss and omit the perle cotton except on picot edging.

A small veil may be made in any color by simply dyeing both tulle and organdy to match.

Contemporary Carrickmacross lace is not as elaborate or as finely made as it was when originally introduced in Ireland in 1820. The tulle was extremely fine and made by hand.

Today, the designs are simpler, with more background showing and the fabrics drip-dry, but the technique is the same and the workmanship is excellent.

Bridal veil, Carrickmacross lace. Author's collection.

Border repeat

Flower

Half-pattern of wreath

SCANDINAVIAN NEEDLEWORK

The arts of weaving and knitting are far more popular in Norway than needle-work. However, the display of needlemade articles at Den Norske Húsfüdsforet-ningen in Oslo was impressive. This is one of several government-sponsored centers in Norway that teach, exhibit, and sell art and crafts. There were needle-made Rye (Rya) rugs in bold, contemporary patterns and counted-thread work such as cross-stitch, straight Gobelin, and needleweaving.

The quality of workmanship is excellent and the designs are almost equally divided between the abstract and folklore whimsy. The colors are fairly consis-tent in the magnificent earth and dark forest tones of the Scandinavian peninsula.

Needleweaving is not typical of any one country but it is handled most attrac-tivly in Norway as in the three samples shown. A length of yarn of a different color or texture from that of the fabric is woven in and out of the existing fabric threads. The weaving motion resembles that of a running stitch. The needle goes over and under a specific (carefully counted) number of threads, and the way in which the working thread is woven determines the ultimate pattern.

The three patterns shown are of Norwegian origin. They are worked in wool yarns on even-weave hand-loomed cloth.

Page 70 shows a small runner with half-pattern. It repeats in mirror image with fringes at both ends. The needleweaving is worked alongside the warp thread of the linen. The center line is a lighter value of the main color, dark red wool yarn. The working thread should be cut to the length of the entire runner so that each strand is woven without knots and is reversible. The cut edges are folded back and slip-stitched neatly. Simple knotted fringes are added in match-ing yarn. See working graph, page 70.

A small pillow top worked in black wool yarn on cream-colored linen is illus-trated and graphed on pages 72–73. Needleweaving is worked alongside warp threads.

The long runner, page 71, is in traditional shades of blue, rust, yellow, and white heavy wool yarn in hand-loomed wool fabric. The needleweaving is worked alongside the weft of the fabric.

Work weave with an even tension and don't pull the threads too tightly. If

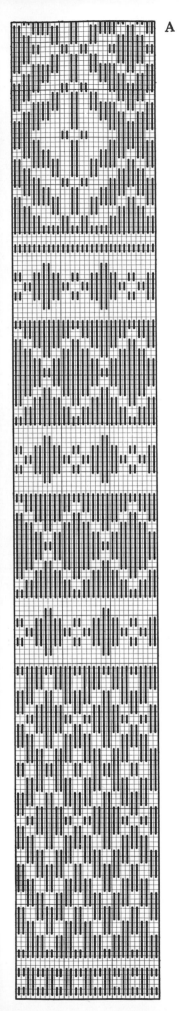

A

Reverse pattern at A for second half of runner

Norwegian runner (half).

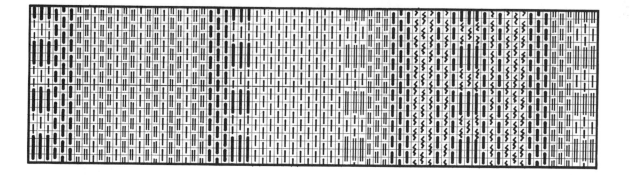

Norwegian runner.

COLOR KEY

⊟ Blue

⊞ Rust

⸨ Yellow

⊟ White

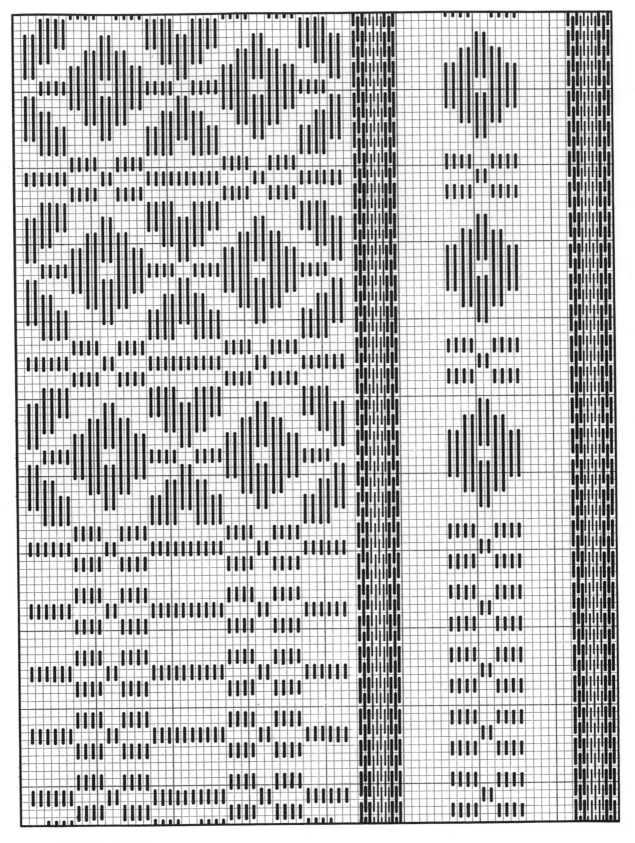

COLOR KEY

Black

White

Norwegian pillow top.

the working thread is too heavy, clip the fabric thread at both ends and draw it out. The heavy needleweaving will fit better and give the finished work a less bulky effect. See working graph, page 71.

In general the needlewoven lines may be worked with a single length of thread which can be measured quite accurately at the start. On a longer piece of fabric such as a skirt hemline, it is possible to use shorter threads and tie the ends with a weaver's knot (see page 65). Do this at irregular intervals so that the knots don't all line up in a row.

Note: All runners may be enlarged with additional rows of needleweaving. The first two designs may be adapted to bargello stitchery.

Detail of fringe for a runner.

Swedish Needlework

Needlework is very popular in Sweden—perhaps the only country where it is taken seriously on all levels: export and import of supplies, conservation of the old designs and techniques, a well-stocked leisure occupation, and some very exciting advances in contemporary work.

There is also a flourishing cottage industry under the sponsorship of the Svensk Hemslöjd. This is a cooperative that handles quality folk crafts including needlework in old regional designs. The most interesting of these are the hand-crafted articles made by the Lapps, an ancient people who live in the far north and who create beautiful and useful articles from leather, reindeer horn, and a strange type of needlework of spun pewter threads couched over brightly colored fabrics in designs that resemble runic signs. This latter technique is attributed exclusively to the Lapps.

It was not possible for me to travel to Lapland to photograph the native techniques, but several patterns from old belts and collars that I saw at the National Museum in Stockholm are reproduced on this page. The symbols may be worked with twisted metallic silver thread couched with waxed embroidery floss. They are most effective on bright red, blue, and green felt or heavy woolen fabric.

The most important contribution to the preservation and the furthering of Swedish needlework was made by the Textile Art Association, the Föreningen Handarbetets Vänner (Friends of Swedish Handicrafts), often abbreviated H.V. During the hundred years of its existence, its members have worked to preserve and maintain the wealth of textile knowledge developed by Swedish women in the preindustrial community.

During the nineteenth century the H.V. imitated Swedish traditional peasant embroideries, concentrating mainly on geometrics, cross-stitch, satin stitch florals, and of course openwork. In the early part of the twentieth century there was a departure from the traditional and a new, rather stylized stitch-oriented technique developed, called Jugend embroidery.

Today Sweden is one of three or four countries in the world where stitchery is accepted as a serious form of art. Many professional artists in other media have experimented with and incorporated yarns and fabrics into their works. The results are truly original and certainly worth a trip to Stockholm during the annual handwork exhibit at the Liljevalchs Museum. There the display of stitch designs and techniques is breathtaking.

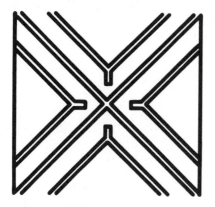

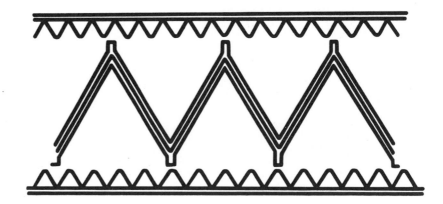

Wall Hangings

In Plate 10 and below are shown two stitchery designs by Kristina Friberg, a contemporary Swedish artist who refers to her work as fabric collage. She uses commercial fabrics of great variety and approaches each project with an open mind. The cutout shapes are pinned to a backing, which in turn is pinned to a wall. This is preferable to pinning the work to a table, because the artist can step back and survey the overall design as it begins to take shape.

It takes hours of work to establish a design. It is then allowed to "rest" for a few days and is reevaluated. Adjustments are made where necessary and the work is removed from the wall, basted carefully, and unpinned.

The design outlines are then embroidered with fanciful stitchery, some to fasten the cutout fabrics to the backing and others to emphasize parts of the design. Any number of stitches and thread textures may be used.

"Butterfly" by Kristina Friberg.

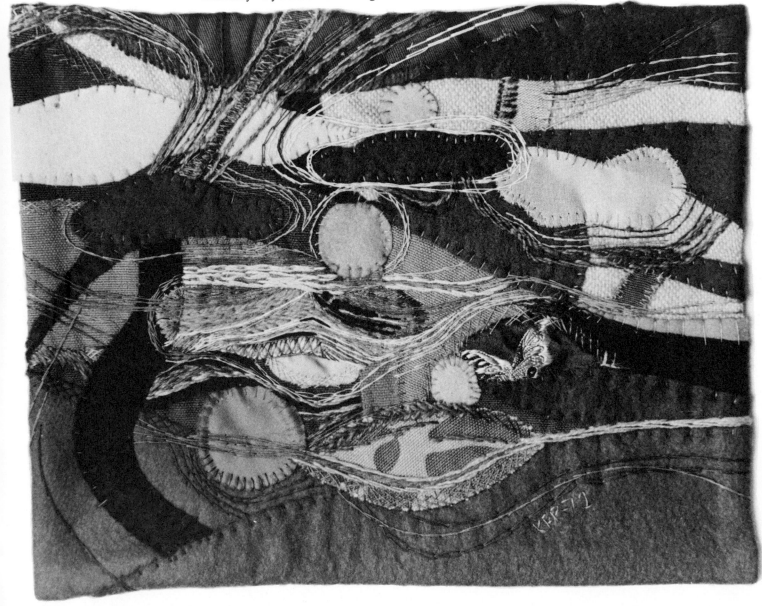

Center motif for jacket

The short jacket and the accessories in Plates 11, 12, and 13 are done in nineteenth-century folk art craft motifs. The designs are simple and relatively easy to reproduce freehand.

The jacket embroidery (above) is worked in long and short, satin, and stem stitches in white, yellow, red, blue, green, and violet wool yarns. It is a nice technique to use on a denim jacket. Draw the flowers and leaves freehand with a fine-tip felt marking pen in an all-over design and embroider with wool, cotton, or rayon embroidery threads.

Jacket and Accessories

Ethnic Dolls

These dolls (Plate 14) were purchased in a boutique in Sweden. They are available with a large variety of ethnic costumes, but the fundamental pattern is the same. The design outline is stamped on a specially striped fabric that delineates the hair, face, upper and lower costume. Notice that the hands fall into the same stripe as the bodice.

INSTRUCTIONS

The doll pattern measures 7 by 12 inches, and the diagram is shown in actual size opposite. Trace upper half of doll pattern on tracing paper with a broken line across the middle. Line up broken line of lower half of pattern and finish the tracing. This is the full pattern outline and is the same for both front and back of dolls.

To simulate stripes, cut them from fabrics of different colors. Measure doll pattern from top of head to middle of forehead, from forehead to neck, from neck to waist, from waist to top of socks, and from socks to tips of shoes or, as in the case of doll number 4, from waist to shoes.

Each strip of fabric should measure 9 inches in width and the appropriate height plus ½ inch for seam allowance. Sew stripes together and press seams flat. The finished rectangles should measure 9 by 14 inches.

The back of the doll is made the same way except that the hair color should extend from top of head to neckline. Copy the costume embroidery on front and back of each doll pattern. This can be done freehand, or the costume patterns may be enlarged to fit inside the basic pattern outline and traced.

Outline each doll with machine stitching at the widest gauge. This will identify the outline on the wrong side. Complete all embroidery. This is mainly stem, chain, long and short, satin, and some lazy daisies. You can improvise if you wish.

Press and line up doll halves along costume embroidery. Place wrong sides out. Pin and then baste together. This is when you will understand the importance of the original machine-stitch outline on the right side of the fabric.

Remove pins and machine stitch carefully all around, leaving an opening at one side. (All stuffed toys should be machine stitched to ensure a smooth and sturdy seamline.)

Cut away fabric around the doll outline, leaving a ¼-inch margin. Clip into corners and around curves *up to* but not *into* the stitching. Turn doll right side out.

Poke out legs and arms gently with a long stick. Stuff with cotton or polyester batting. Use small bits of filler and stuff firmly with a stick or the blunt end of a knitting needle. Fold in opening and sew it closed with tiny stitches.

Pummel and pull the doll to distribute stuffing and improve its shape if necessary. Doll's hair is embroidered along with the costume. Girl dolls, however, have an additional fringe above the ears. This is tacked on after the doll is finished and either left to hang straight or twisted into a loop and tacked. Clip ends even.

Note: The dolls may be embroidered on a single unstriped fabric of any color. Improvise costumes and color combinations but use the same doll pattern.

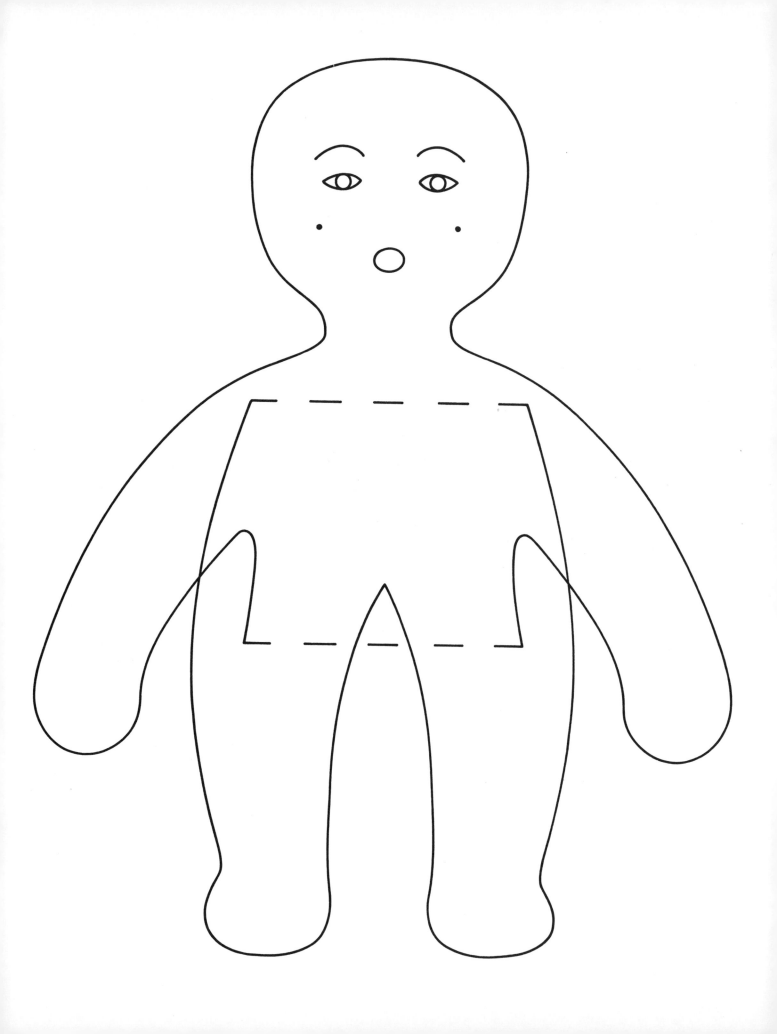

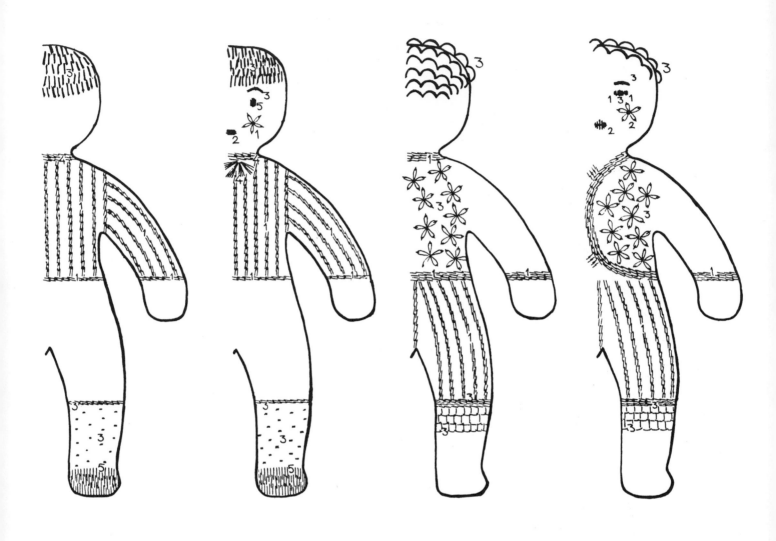

DOLL 1
COLOR KEY
1 = Orange
2 = Red
3 = Dark red
4 = Blue
5 = Black

DOLL 2
COLOR KEY
1 = White
2 = Red
3 = Black

80

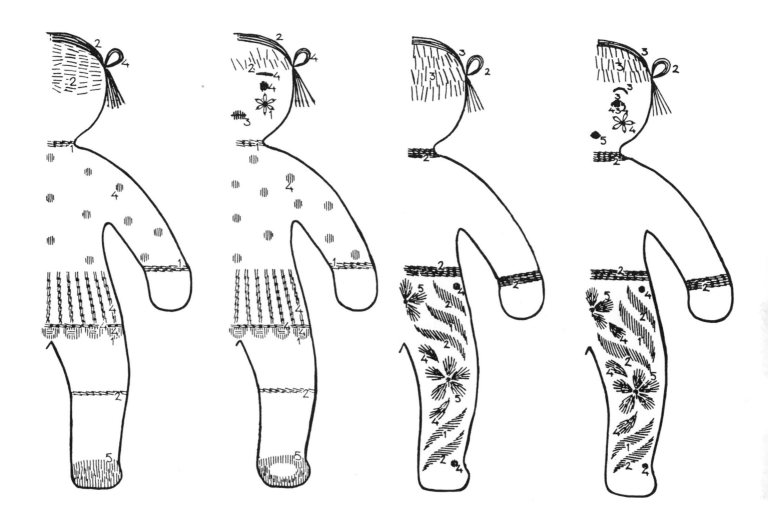

DOLL 3
COLOR KEY
1 = White
2 = Orange
3 = Red
4 = Turquoise
5 = Black

DOLL 4
COLOR KEY
1 = Light green
2 = Medium green
3 = Navy blue
4 = Pink
5 = Red

81

DANISH NEEDLEWORK

Denmark is one of the most important export centers of needlework supplies in the world. Some of the finest embroidery linens, even-weave cotton, canvas, and yarns are now imported from Denmark.

Two of its largest distributors, O. Oehlenschlagers and Carl J. Permin, export an impressive selection of embroidery fabrics, smooth tapestry yarn, and top-quality counted-stitch patterns for pillows, wall hangings, bell pulls, and assorted accessories (see list of suppliers, page 178).

Oehlenschlagers stocks several hundred fabrics in assorted qualities and colors, including needlepoint canvas in shades of red, blue, green, orange, gray, brown, and lavender (to mention only a few).

The Permin Zephir tapestry wool is a smooth, four-ply yarn that separates easily and is ideal for work on counted-thread designs.

The Danish counted-thread patterns are usually printed in color and are therefore easier to read than those printed in black and white. They are generally worked in cross-stitch.

Samples of patterns are shown on the next three pages. The standard graph paper count is twenty squares to the inch, one cross-stitch per square. To enlarge a pattern, select a fabric in a large gauge.

Divide fabric in quarters by working a running stitch in contrasting thread in a vertical and horizontal line through the center point. Work one-quarter of the pattern at a time, counting the threads from the center line outward.

The design shown opposite may be enlarged as a small rug or wall hanging and worked on number 10 or even number 5 double-thread canvas. Work with appropriate yarns in single or double cross-stitch. The design is effective when worked in two colors such as red and white.

The "Rose Vine" bell pull (pages 84–85) may also be enlarged on number 10 or number 5 double-thread canvas. Work two or more complete strips, add a black background, and piece them along the edges to form an attractive area rug or a runner.

Note: Should you decide to work in half cross-stitch to save time, use heavier yarn and the basketweave technique. Narrow strips will never block properly if they are distorted with the continental stitch.

Here is a helpful hint for those who are uneasy about facing a large piece of blank canvas in counted-stitch work. Divide the entire surface of the canvas into squares by drawing horizontal and vertical lines on every tenth thread of the canvas.

Use a yardstick and a black acrylic marking pen. Draw lines right on the canvas threads; on Penelope canvas count the two threads as one.

Bear in mind that although the stitches are indicated in graph squares, they are worked over the threads or mesh of the canvas.

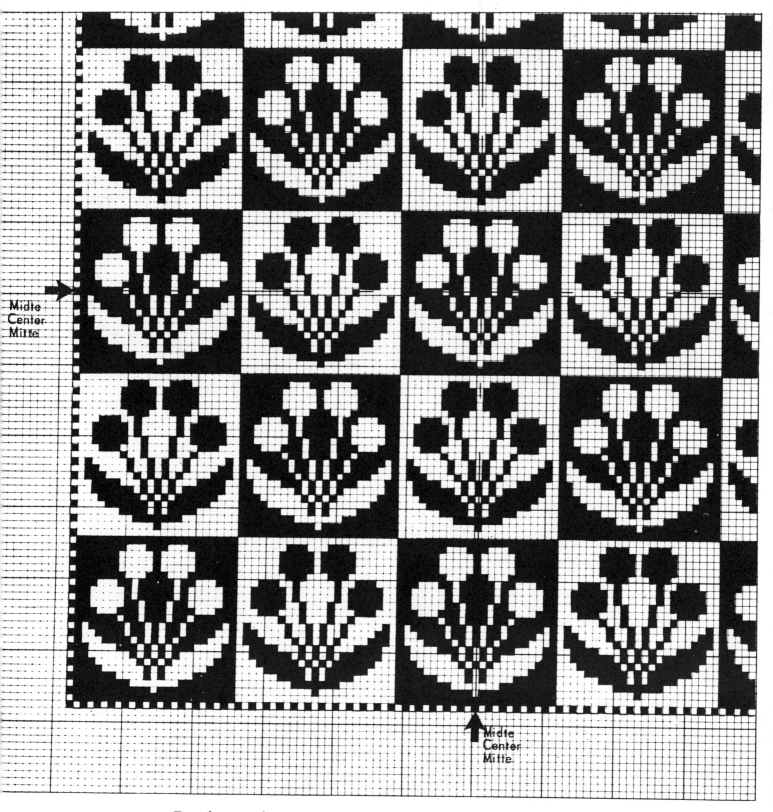

Midte
Center
Mitte

Midte
Center
Mitte

Danish two-color cross-stitch pattern. Design by Carl J. Permin.

COLOR KEY

Roses: five shades of red; darkest is deep wine, indicated in black; lightest is pale rose, indicated in white.

Danish counted-thread "Rose Vine" bell pull. Design by Carl J. Permin.

Leaves and stems: four shades of green; select compatible colors.

ark 2.

mønsteret fortsættes her

"Peepers." Wall hanging, 35 by 55 centimeters. Linen threads on linen fabric, white, beige, brown, blue, green. Designed by Irmelin Grönlund and worked by Friends of Finnish Handicraft.

FINNISH NEEDLEWORK

Contemporary Finnish needlework is low-keyed and charming. It is surprisingly different in concept from that of other European countries.

Instead of using a variety of stitches to create a design, the new school of thought in Finland is that one basic stitch can be worked to create shadows, textures, outlines, and flat filled areas.

This is the universal stem stitch, one of the simplest of embroidery stitches. Yet, the stitchery isn't as simple as it sounds. In fact, it places a greater demand on your skills and ability to interpret a design and color blends. The result is light and airy and very easy to live with.

I loved the embroideries at Suomen Kasityon Ystavat Oy (Friends of Finnish Handicraft) in Helsinki, where I selected three designs, shown on pages 86 and 88 and in Plate 15. One is based on an old stylized Finnish folk pattern and the other two are contemporary.

All are embroidered with a simple, rather large and casual stem stitch that seems to be used as a brush stroke.

GENERAL INSTRUCTIONS

The outlines are easy to duplicate and enlarge from the photographs (see enlarging instructions, pages 8–9). Practice the stem stitch (page 170) in straight and curvilinear outlines. Stitches should be fairly large and open, the needle coming out pretty close to the point of entrance; and the wrong side should not look like backstitch.

To fill in larger areas, study Plate 15, "My Horse." The stitches are used as brush strokes and not in circular outline. (This would also make a lovely appliqué pattern, somewhat in the style of the Dahomey work, page 128.)

No special effort is made to cover fabric completely, and the small spaces where it peeks through add a lightness to the overall design. Thread and fabric in these samples are all linen, but you may use cotton embroidery floss or fine crewel wool and just about any fabric of good quality.

"My Horse." Wall hanging, 40 by 60 centimeters. Linen threads on linen. Designed by Mirja Tissari and worked by Friends of Finnish Handicraft. (See Plate 15.)

"Rattlesnake." Linen pillow, black on beige, 40 by 45 centimeters. Designed by Airi Snellman-Hänninen and worked by Friends of Finnish Handicraft.

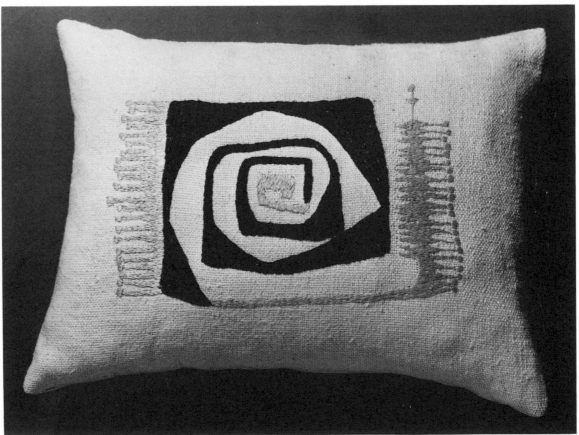

DUTCH NEEDLEWORK

When I started to work on this book, I promised myself that I would use only examples of needlework that could be clearly understood. I would refrain from using "museum pieces" unless they were pertinent and the technique could be explained easily. In showing you the needlework in Plate 16 I am not sure that I have kept my promise, but I know that I would never forgive myself if I failed to share this magnificent discovery with my readers.

It was hidden in a remote corner of the doll house exhibit at the Rijksmuseum in Amsterdam: a needlepainting signed by W. Haelweck and dated 1650.

In the early part of the seventeenth century in Holland, there was a group of artists who worked with needle and thread. They called themselves needlepainters, and if this example is any indication of their work, they must have been remarkable indeed.

According to the museum director, this is the only remaining needlepainting known to be in existence from that era. It is reproduced here for the first time through the courtesy of the Rijksmuseum.

Because of the intricacy of the design and color blends, it was impossible to work out a color key. I can only tell you that it measures 36 by 51 centimeters and is worked entirely in small straight stitches with fine silk thread on a satin backing (see diagram, page 90). Without exception, it is the most magnificent piece of needlework I have ever seen.

Contemporary needlework is very popular in Holland and the range of the craft is wide. There are enormous "things" stuffed with batting and huge string works that are so complicated that even the artist cannot remember how they were made. This is true of most countries where needlework is undergoing a transformation.

White Work

I was impressed with some of the charming white work and I selected one example by N. Breeuer-Kaal. Her designs are restrained and show a fine quality of workmanship with special attention to detail.

Study the photograph on page 92 and the closeup on page 93. Notice how stitches and threads are utilized to develop a design. Small backstitches form an outline for trapunto padding. The same backstitches, pulled tightly, create the open areas. Long stitches worked close together produce the shadings, and shiny threads are used for highlights.

Outline for Dutch needlepainting shown in Plate 16.

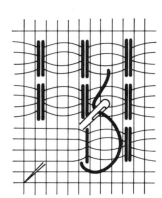

INSTRUCTIONS

The actual size of the embroidery is 11 by 14 inches, including the border. It is worked on fine, closely woven linen with several shades of linen thread in white, off-white, bone, cream, and eggshell, both mat and polished.

The stitches used are pulled-thread (right), running (page 170), long and short (page 171), french knots (page 174), backstitch (page 170), and eyelet (page 173). Some areas are padded in trapunto or light quilting.

Materials

 17-by-21-inch piece of embroidery linen of good quality
 One skein each of linen or cotton embroidery threads in a selection of textures and shades mentioned above
 Sharp embroidery needles to accommodate the various threads

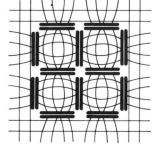

Dutch white work,
designed and worked
by N. Breeuer-Kaal.

You will also need a frame with 14-by-17-inch inner dimension to allow a 3-inch space above design border. (Instructions for building a frame are on page 7.)

Enlarge diagram on page 91 and transfer it onto pressed fabric. Line with a piece of sheer fabric such as organdy or lawn in the same size and stretch both on the frame. There should be a 3-inch border allowance inside the frame, and the rest of the fabric is to be folded over and stapled firmly around the frame.

Work all stitches through both fabrics, beginning from the center. Study detail photograph opposite and stitch details on pages 91 and 170–174.

Stitches are simple, and the overall feeling is light and airy. The shades and textures of the various threads are arbitrary and should be determined by the individual. This is not a kit, after all, and some personal interpretation is always recommended.

To pad in trapunto, slit the lining in the areas where padding is indicated. Insert bits of cotton or polyester fluff with a thin stick or crochet hook. Pad lightly and close the slit with a few stitches.

Note: This design may be enlarged considerably and worked with heavier threads on coarser fabric. See general information on enlarging and transferring patterns on pages 8–11.

Detail of white work.

HUNGARIAN NEEDLEWORK

In Hungary, needlework is a very prosperous cottage industry under the auspices of the Hungarian Cooperative Trading Company. Better known under its trade name, Hungarocoop, it controls at this time twenty needlework cooperatives. Each of these represents a specific region and a particular style and color scheme.

The most famous of the cooperatives are Matyo, Bereg, Hodmezovasarhely Heves, Buznak, Karag, and Kalocsa.

When I was in Hungary I visited Kalocsa, a tiny village a four-hour bus ride from Budapest. The cooperative headquarters was in a large old farmhouse built in the early part of the eighteenth century. The flowers painted on the walls are the same as those on the embroideries and are the stock-in-trade of the Kalocsa design.

The polychrome floral designs of Kalocsa are some of the most popular of the European folk art embroideries and the ones most specifically identified as Hungarian. I think they are lovely and quite easy to reproduce, since all they require is a simple satin stitch and colorful cotton embroidery thread.

The cooperatives employ a large work force of girls and women who produce vast amounts of tablecloths, blouses, vests, shawls, pillowcases, and anything else that would interest the consumer market. Hungarian embroideries are exported all over the world and are quite expensive. Since this is essentially a profit-making venture, expedience often takes precedence over individual creativity. As in most cottage industries, there is a sameness about the embroideries, a kind of mass production, and original pieces of work are uncommon. Still, a standard of quality is maintained, and the merchandise is not shoddy.

I brought several embroideries from Hungary. They represent various cooperatives and differ considerably in style and technique. The designs are adaptable to any number of articles from vests to pillows to tablecloths or place mats.

Tablecloth

The tablecloth in Plate 17 measures 66 by 84 inches. There is a small center rosette, and on each half of the cloth there are three individual patterns flowing toward the center. The large patterns are shown in color in Plate 18 and the cor-

Center motif

Center

Middle motif   Center

Bottom motif

Center

responding diagrams are shown on pages 95, 96, and 97. The rosettes are diagrammed below. One-half of the tablecloth is photographed showing the direction of the design toward the center. The other half would face in the opposite direction.

Each individual pattern measures 11 by 14 inches in actual size. The center rosette is 2½ inches in diameter.

Enlarge patterns according to the general instructions on pages 8–9. Decide on the size of tablecloth desired and purchase the appropriate amount of fabric, preferably of a drip-dry variety. If you want a smaller cloth than the one shown, delete the corresponding patterns. For a larger cloth, add one or more of the patterns at each end. A small square cloth looks good with four patterns, one on each of the four sides, and a rosette in the center.

Work in satin stitch (page 170), following color key in diagrams (below) and color plates. The smaller flower details are scattered along the border and placed in the corners of napkins. Work neatly and bury all tail ends under worked areas on the wrong side. Each petal, center, bud, and leaf is worked in satin stitch. The stems, if any, are worked in stem stitch (page 170).

COLOR KEY

1 = Medium green
2 = Dark green
3 = Light red
4 = Dark red
5 = Yellow
6 = Light yellow
7 = Orange
8 = Pink

9 = Light purple
10 = Dark purple
11 = Medium lavender
12 = Light lavender
13 = Medium green
14 = Light blue
15 = Medium blue
16 = Light orange

The women in Kalocsa don't use embroidery hoops, but you may use one if you are accustomed to it. The border is worked in machine eyelet. This is very time-consuming if done by hand and has a tendency to fray after several washings.

I recommend a folded hem at least 2½ inches deep with mitered corners. Draw a thread on all four sides to get a nice straight line and work a favorite hemming stitch. Work the napkins the same way but with a narrower hem, and don't forget to account for the hemline when purchasing fabric.

Cutwork

One of the most attractive and original European folk-style embroideries is the Kalocsa cutwork (Plate 19). Originally it was made entirely by hand. The design was transferred to a piece of cotton embroidery fabric. The satin stitch was worked in the hand, then the entire piece was pinned to a frame and the open-work was finished with cutwork and pulled-thread stitches.

Today, the lace work is done by machine. The changeover is regrettable, especially when the old is compared with the new. When I visited the Kalocsa co-operative I was able to observe the machine work in progress. After the flowers have been embroidered, the piece is taken over by another group of workers who use very sophisticated machines to create the intricate lace work.

The outline of the lace design is transferred along with the flower pattern and couched with a double thread. The satin stitch embroidery is also outlined with couching. The machine completes the couching, and the centers are cut out by hand. The large openings are filled in with the most incredible "spider work." All this is done with the speed of lightning.

I must admit that I was very impressed with the machine operator, whose skill was certainly superior to that of some of the hand workers. The general effect may be duplicated as follows.

INSTRUCTIONS

Create a square of lace by assembling an assortment of lace fabric and inserts. Pieces of old lace are ideal. Pin them to a sheet of heavy tracing paper, over-lapping edges as you go. The actual size of the lace work is 24 by 24 inches, but you can make it any size. Baste and remove pins.

Machine stitch lace pieces through the paper. Don't remove paper, because it gives the lace body.

Transfer the flower patterns (page 100) to a 24-inch square of cotton fabric (see general directions, pages 9–11), position it over the lace square, and baste. Pin both fabrics to a frame large enough to encompass the entire design outline. Outline the flowers with a close buttonhole stitch (page 175) and fill in centers with satin stitch (page 170). Work with three strands of the six-strand embroidery floss and go over the design carefully to cover the lace.

Remove from frame. Peel away paper on the reverse side and cut away excess cotton fabric close to the buttonhole outline with very sharp scissors to expose the lace.

On all work use D.M.C. or Coats & Clark six-strand cotton embroidery floss in colors indicated.

Center motif

One-quarter center motif

The embroideries of the Matyo cooperative resemble those of Kalocsa except that they are worked on a black background and are most often seen on vests, wall hangings, and shawls. Red, bright pink, peacock blue, and green predominate.

The vest shown in Plate 20 may be reproduced on any simple commercial pattern. The fabric is felt and needs no interfacing or lining. The design (below) should be transferred with white dressmaker's carbon. If the transfer does not register, pin the tracing-paper pattern to felt and machine stitch design outline through paper with bright thread. Remove paper and embroider, covering stitched outline as you work.

Other Embroideries

COLOR KEY

1 = Light green
2 = Dark green
3 = Pink
4 = Red
5 = Purple
6 = Plum
7 = Blue
8 = Gold
9 = Orange

Center

The striking pillow top in Plate 21 can be enlarged to make a small rug or wall hanging. The diagram outline (above) is a quarter pattern and indicates design placement rather than detail. The flower petals and small circlets within circlets should be drawn freehand on the tracing paper. This will facilitate individual adjustment to the intricacies of this pattern.

Matyo embroideries look best when worked with shiny threads.

102

Felt appliqué (see page 14) is worked nearly always in red and black. One color is cut out like a fancy paper doily and placed on the second, which serves as a background. Stitching is done by hand or machine; and since the fabric is always felt, there is no need for folding under.

Hungarian felt appliqué.

Center

Hungarian cross-stitch. See Plate 24.

The two cross-stitch patterns shown on page 107 are from Bereg. Cross-stitch is almost classic in European embroidery, and there is hardly a country that does not have some designs featuring it in counted-thread stitchery.

You will find simple designs like this very useful. Enlarged, they may be worked on canvas with wool yarns and are very attractive as borders on practically anything.

105

Hungarian cross-stitch. See Plate 24.

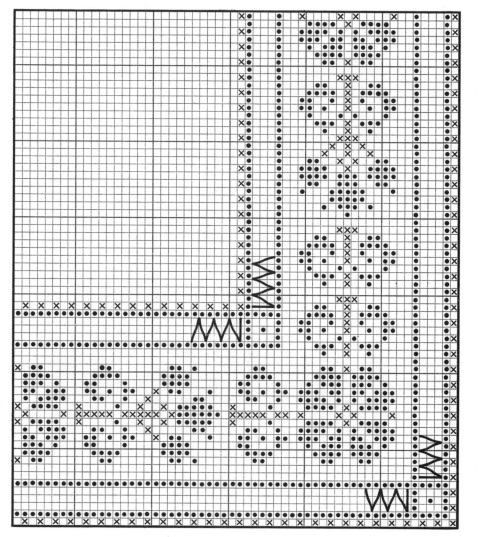

COLOR KEY

- ⊡ Red
- ⊠ Black

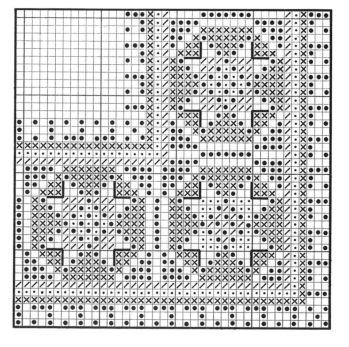

COLOR KEY

- ⊡ Black
- ⊠ Red
- ⊿ Green
- ▫ Yellow

Hungarian embroidered square. See Plate 24.

The embroidered square, above—a charming stylized design worked in cross-stitch (page 172), chain (page 171), and open buttonhole (page 175)—is from Buzsak. The colors are black and red on natural linen, which is a popular color combination in folk craft throughout Europe.

One-quarter pattern
1 = Black (heavy line)
2 = Red (fine line)

RUMANIAN NEEDLEWORK

Rumania is the only country in Europe at this time where the manufacture of national costumes is a successful cottage industry. The embroidery and costume designs are copied from old patterns, and the regional styles and colors are controlled by strict guidelines.

Rumanian national costumes are some of the most beautiful in the world, and the women's blouses are lavishly embroidered. The patterns are geometric and worked in counted-thread cross-stitch or Holbein outline. They adapt perfectly to the basic construction of the blouse, which is made up of four rectangular pieces of fabric.

The structure of the Rumanian costume dates back to the pre-Christian era when the Dacians occupied the geographical area north of the Danube that is now Rumania. Dacia was conquered by the Roman Empire and in turn by Tartars and the Turks. It was divided by the Hungarians, Austrians, and Russians and was reunited in turns.

The Rumanian language and customs underwent many changes, yet most of the national costumes remain virtually unchanged and structured along the same ancient lines and geometric embroidery. This is recorded iconographically in the carved stone images of ancient Roman monuments such as the Tropaeum Trajani from Adamklissi in Dobrudja and Trajan's Column in Rome.

The embroidery threads are generally red and black. Occasionally there is some blue, green, or yellow with black outline. Polychrome is not traditional in costume embroidery and is the exception rather than the rule. Basic costume fabric is always white.

As in most European countries, needlework is a very popular way of decorating just about anything that would take a threaded needle. So one finds embroidered tablecloths, towels, wall hangings, leather clothing, and accessories resplendent with embroidery. There is appliqué, bead and metal ornamentation, and of course a great deal of drawnwork in both color and white on white.

The most dramatic embroidery is reserved for women's costumes. In some districts the entire blouse may be covered with an elaborate pattern of cross-stitch embroidery worked on their very fine *pânza-de-in*, or linen cloth. A woman of wealth might add beads and sequins to the embroidery for a touch of elegance but with strict adherence to regional design guidelines.

A fine example of such beaded embroidery follows.

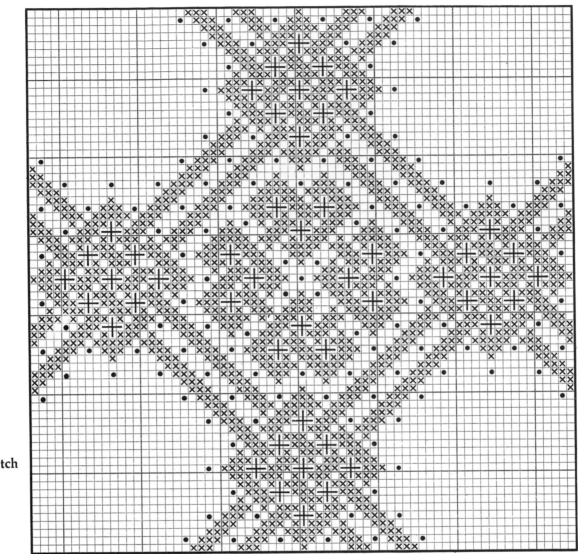

KEY

+   Beads

•   Sequins

×   Cross-stitch

Beaded Design on Girl's Blouse

The beaded shirt in Plate 22 dates back to the late eighteenth or early nineteenth century. It looks very elaborate but is actually based on a small repeat pattern (see the graph above).

INSTRUCTIONS

Materials

    Small glass beads in colors indicated (see Plate 23)
    Small crystal beads
    Silver-colored sequins
    Strong sewing thread
    Black six-strand embroidery floss or any black embroidery thread compatible with your fabric
    Beading or fine darning needle
    Embroiderer's wax
    Embroidery frame

110

The amount of beads and sequins needed will depend on the size of the embroidery. Glass beads are available at craft shops and may be purchased in small packets. The color range is very good; and, although it may be difficult to match the antique shades accurately, the selection should be large enough for a lovely color blend.

Buy a small amount in every color. Colored beads should be opaque and white beads crystal clear. The gauge is very important. The beads should fit over one thread and the sequins over four threads of the fabric you select. Bring a piece of fabric along when purchasing the beads.

Fabric should be a good-quality even-weave linen with a fairly large gauge for the initial sample. Work up a few square inches and then make a decision about a larger project.

To begin, study the graph opposite. The main outline is shown in small crosses and should be worked first in cross-stitch using a black embroidery thread compatible with your fabric.

The colored beads are indicated with large crosses. Bring the threaded needle into the top of the cross, string five beads of one color on the needle, slide them onto the thread, and bring needle over to the bottom of the cross and to the wrong side. The beads should lie flat and fill the line. If not, add or remove one or more beads as needed. Bring needle out to the left of the cross and string the same number of beads on the needle. Bring needle to the right and complete the beaded cross. Take a small stitch on the underside before moving on to the next cross. This prevents the beads from shifting too much. Follow color placement by checking the color plate.

Sequins are indicated with dots on the graph outline. Sew them on by bringing the threaded needle through center hole of sequin. String small crystal bead and bring needle back through the same sequin center. Repeat with enough sequins to cover the immediate area of the small pattern. Fasten thread on the wrong side with several stitches taken right under the sequins.

Wax thread slightly and fasten tail end securely. It is recommended that beads and sequins be sewn to fabric in small batches. This is in case one should become loose; then only a small section of the embroidery would be affected.

The colored beads may be replaced with large cross-stitches worked on a heavier thread and in the appropriate colors.

This embroidery design is very rich, and a little goes a long way. It is excellent for use in borders, sleeves, neckline ornaments, and handbags. The cross-stitch may be worked in the hand, but all beading and sequin work should be done on a frame.

Bessarabian Shirts

The embroidered shirts on page 112 are from Bessarabia and are typical of the festival costumes worn by men in the rural areas in the early part of the twentieth century.

The province of Bessarabia was annexed to Rumania after World War I, and for the next thirty years the local embroideries, especially on shirts and blouses, were very popular.

Russian design elements prevailed on occasion: for example, the flower cross-stitch pattern is Russian, whereas the geometric one is Rumanian.

Embroidered shirts from Bessarabia. See Plate 24. Author's collection.

Shirt construction, with the fold-back collar and front opening, is Rumanian. Russian shirts (*rubajky*) have side openings and a narrow band instead of a collar.

The shirt pattern is reproduced opposite for those interested in making an authentic Rumanian peasant shirt.

INSTRUCTIONS

Materials

   4 yards of even-weave embroidery linen, 45 inches wide
   12 skeins each of red and black six-strand cotton embroidery floss

The pattern size is medium.

Enlarge pattern according to general instructions on pages 8–9. Trace outline on tracing paper. Press linen fabric and position the patterns on it so that the selvage runs vertically. Transfer the front, back, and sleeves (outlines) to four rectangles of fabric. Transfer collar, cuffs, and gusset on another rectangle, leaving enough space between them for cutting out and stitching.

The embroidery must be worked before the pattern is assembled. If the rectangles of fabric have a tendency to ravel, machine stitch a border around each.

112

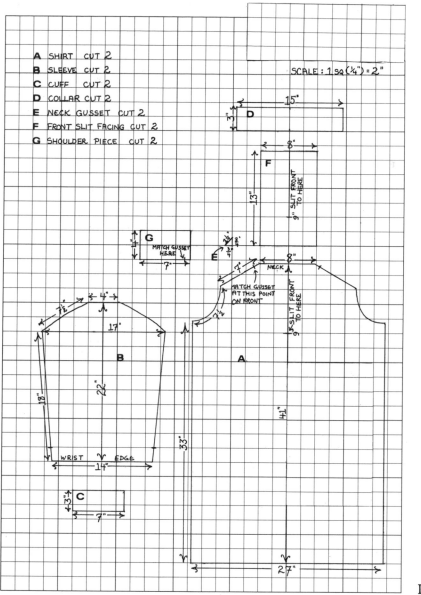

A | SHIRT CUT 2
B | SLEEVE CUT 2
C | CUFF CUT 2
D | COLLAR CUT 2
E | NECK GUSSET CUT 2
F | FRONT SLIT FACING CUT 2
G | SHOULDER PIECE CUT 2

SCALE : 1 SQ (¼") = 2"

Pattern by Carol Peretz.

The embroidery layout is shown on page 114. However, the number of patterns will depend on the linen gauge. I recommend that you work up a full pattern on a small piece of your fabric and use it as a gauge for pattern placement (see Plate 24).

The embroidery is worked on the front of the shirt, inside the collar and inter-facing, on the shoulders, cuffs, and the entire sleeve. Whether or not you work all the embroidery is a matter of personal preference. This project, however, re-quires a good knowledge of counted-thread needlework and sewing expertise. It is not recommended for beginners.

When the embroidery is completed, cut out the component parts of the shirt pattern from within the rectangles and stitch together, following outline instruc-tions from pattern.

113

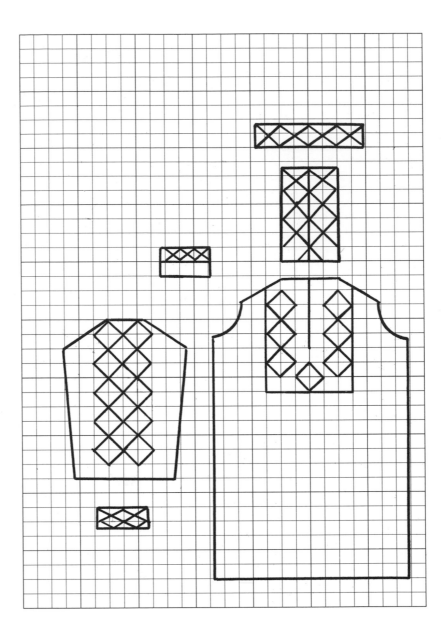

Note: The gusset marked *G* on the diagram fits across the shoulder connecting front and back parts of the shirt. It serves to enlarge the armhole at the top of the sleeve opening.

The collar should be embroidered on the inside only. It will be worn folded back and needs no embroidery on the underside. The 14-inch wrist edge on the sleeve is made to accommodate the 7-inch cuff by making a few small pleats instead of gathers. The cuff is fastened with one button and buttonhole.

The traditional shirt of this kind has no center front seam and has a tendency to look a little baggy unless tied with a sash.

COLOR KEY
☑1 Red
☉2 Black

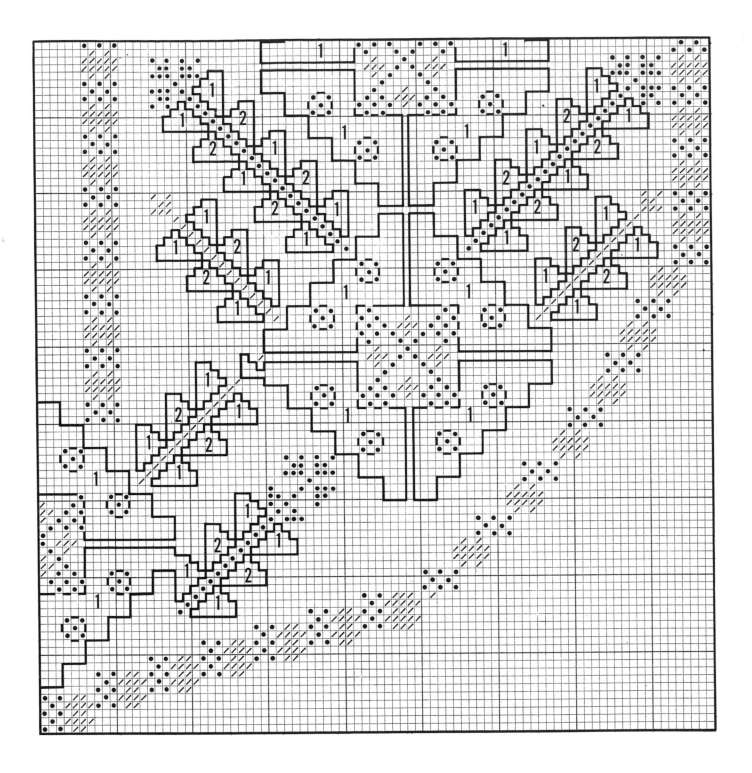

COLOR KEY
☑ 1 Red
⊡ 2 Black

GUATEMALAN NEEDLEWORK

The countryside of Guatemala vibrates with the colors of ethnic costumes worn by both men and women. Each village has its own identifiable style, although there may be variations in the quality of the work as well as in the designs.

The Guatemalans are descendants of the ancient Maya, and the mainstay of their crafts continues to be the weaving techniques of their ancestors. Needlework came much later, probably as a kind of less expensive or less time-consuming way to decorate a costume.

It may have been a thrifty way of using up bits and pieces of thread left over from the weaving looms. Indeed, some of the embroideries look as if there was never enough thread to finish one design. One often sees a flower with four and a half blue petals and the remaining half in red or yellow. The stitches are simple—chain, stem, and a very random type of satin stitch—but the effect is charming and unique.

The designs, carried over from age-old traditions, are symbolic and stylized. Often the designs are limited to the restrictions imposed by the very nature of weaving, which confines threads to angular rather than curvilinear lines. Needlework affords more freedom in design outline, but Guatemalan needlework can always be identified by the loomed patterns.

Huipils

One of the principal articles of clothing of the Maya woman is the *huipil*. It is essentially a rectangle of fabric, folded in half with seams down the sides. The seams are opened at the top to permit the arms to go through, and a hole is cut out on the center fold for the head. Dimensions vary from one village to another, but they nearly always have the general shape of a pillowcase.

Tribal tradition is the guideline for the designs, colors, and size of the *huipil*, and no self-respecting woman from one village would wear the *huipil* of another.

The two *huipils* on page 118 are from two different villages. The one with embroidered collar and cuffs, from Joyabaj, is based on an ancient design symbolic of the sun and its rays. The *huipil* with flowered border is from Santa Barbara and is more or less contemporary. It is worked in chain (page 171), stem (page 170), and satin stitches (page 170) in very bright colors, and the design may be adapted to any blouse top or skirt border. The design diagrams are shown on pages 119–121; they can also be drawn freehand.

117

The neckline ornament shown in Plate 25 is from Quetzaltenango and is embroidered separately and sewn onto the blouse top. This type of neckline is rather modern and is not the customary method of constructing a *huipil*. I selected this one for its interesting variegated colors used to create a shaded effect.

Variegated threads are available in skeins that are dyed in several shades of one color. The chromatic sequence is repeated exactly the same way throughout the length of the thread. In order to make the most of such shading, it is important to understand the design, the types of stitches, and the length of thread in each shade.

No special care is taken in this particular embroidery. The colors are worked arbitrarily, and the shades fall where they may. Still, coupled with the naive design, it has a certain charm and it could be used as a small frame.

The design may be embroidered in solid colors and outlined in black chain or stem stitch for an interesting stained glass effect.

All the Guatemalan embroideries illustrated are worked in a rather off-beat satin stitch, with the exception of the flower-bordered *huipil* from Santa Barbara, where the stem outlines are worked in chain and stem stitch.

Cotton threads are used throughout. Stitchery is worked in the hand rather than on a frame; and if the first row of stitches fails to cover the fabric completely, a return row is worked to cover the empty spaces. Bright colors and bold design take precedence over exactitude of stitchery.

Tops of two *huipils*. Guatemala. Courtesy Mr. Copeland H. Marks.

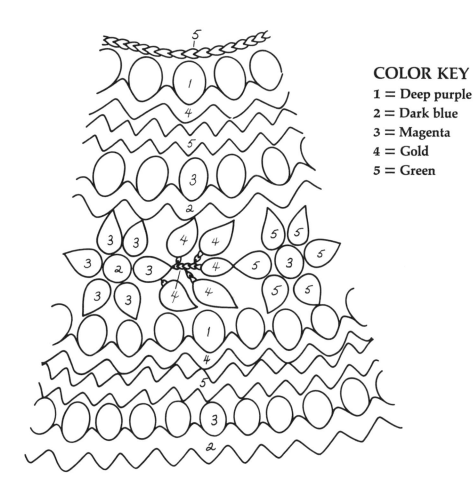

COLOR KEY

1 = Deep purple
2 = Dark blue
3 = Magenta
4 = Gold
5 = Green

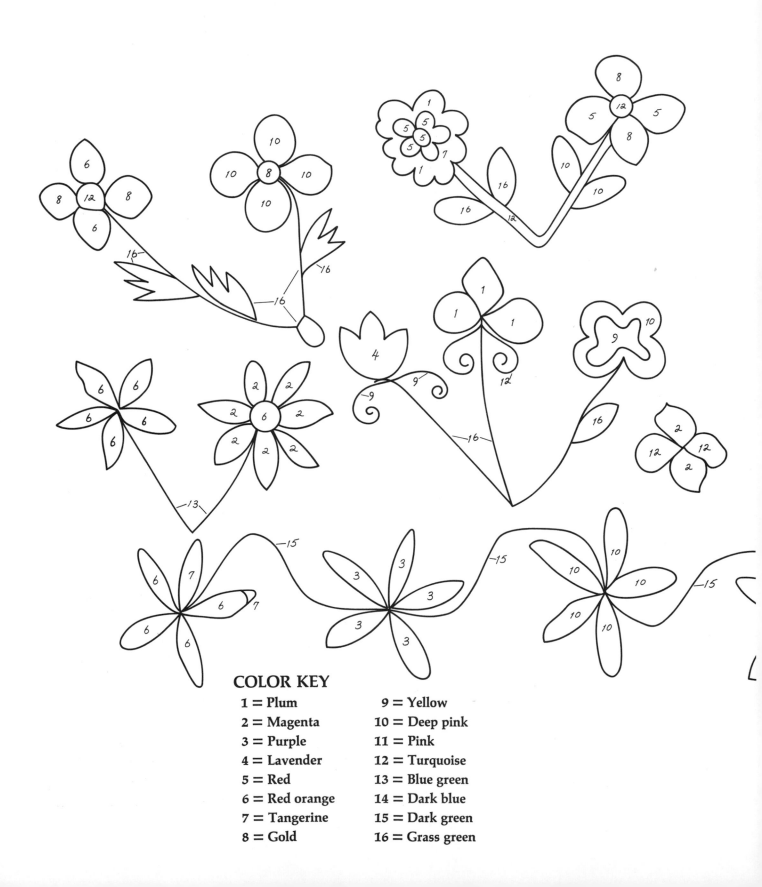

COLOR KEY

1 = Plum	**9** = Yellow
2 = Magenta	**10** = Deep pink
3 = Purple	**11** = Pink
4 = Lavender	**12** = Turquoise
5 = Red	**13** = Blue green
6 = Red orange	**14** = Dark blue
7 = Tangerine	**15** = Dark green
8 = Gold	**16** = Grass green

The result is original native embroidery, an art that is fast disappearing in this tourist-oriented world. The articles from Guatemala were made by individual women for their own use and not purchased in stores.

GENERAL INSTRUCTIONS

Diagrams for design outlines are shown on page 119. Enlarge to any size or use them as is. They make very attractive borders on skirts, blouses, picture frames, curtains, and so forth.

The threads are cotton, but you can use any yarns on appropriate fabrics. Work with close satin stitch and if coverage seems thin, work a second or even a third row to fill in where you missed. Use a frame or embroidery hoop for best results.

San Mateo Altar Cloth

The San Mateo cloth from Ixtatan (Plate 26) is most representative of the colorful needlework of Guatemala. This is the symbolic sun and moon pattern that is most often used to decorate *huipils*, blankets, and altar cloths in this village.

In the hills of Guatemala where the climate is cold, the embroidery on blankets and *huipils* is worked on a double layer of fabric for extra warmth. In other parts of the world clothing and bed covers are quilted for the same reason.

INSTRUCTIONS

To duplicate the cloth shown opposite you will need two single bed sheets and several skeins of cotton embroidery floss in red, magenta, green, black, blue, turquoise, orange, and yellow. Any combination of bright colors may be used as long as they are compatible.

The amount of yarn needed depends on size of stitches and thickness of embroidery. Purchase several skeins in each color and see how far they take you.

Enlarge and trace diagram on page 125 on top sheet. Use diagram as repeat pattern or draw it freehand with a fine marking pen. For a better understanding of the total pattern, examine the photographs. Plate 26 is a partial view of the cloth and serves to indicate color placement. The black-and-white photograph opposite shows the entire work on the right side; and that on page 124 is the reverse side. Work in satin stitch (page 170) in an over-and-under motion. If thread does not cover fabric completely, fill in empty spots with a return row.

The widest bands of magenta are worked as in laid work. The thread is carried across the face of the fabric in one long line, the needle brought to the underside and out again adjacent to the point of entrance, and then carried across the fabric again (see stitch detail, page 174). Allow a space between the stitches and fill them in on a return row. You might have to do this three or four times for full coverage, since cotton does not fluff out like wool yarn and has a tendency to twist.

By placing the wide bands of hot color on the right side of the work, the cloth becomes reversible. The right side is more vibrant and the reverse side, with its unworked areas, more subdued and vaguely reminiscent of early American patchwork.

The striped embroidery is achieved with one color worked a few stitches and a space left at regular intervals to be filled with another color on the return row.

The San Mateo cloth may be enlarged to any size and worked on a single layer of heavier fabric. The overall size of this one is 64 by 68 inches.

Altar cloth from San Mateo, Guatemala. Author's collection.

Detail of altar cloth.

SAN BLAS APPLIQUÉ

The small island of San Blas in Central America is well known for its multi-colored *mola* worked in very intricate reverse appliqué.

The squares of fabric are layered and basted together. The design is outlined on the topmost fabric and then cut through one, two, or more layers to reveal the underlying colors as dictated by the artist's wish.

San Blas appliqué requires great skill, and the vibrating colors are very difficult to work with. The appliqué opposite is unique in its two-color assembly.

The colors vibrate, to be sure. One is a strong magenta and the other a bright turquoise. However, it may be toned down with two earth colors or a combination of black plus any color.

Try black and gray and outline the appliqué with chain stitch (page 171) worked in stark white. This design is simple to reproduce and may be enlarged to any size.

INSTRUCTIONS

Materials

Two compatible shades of fabric. Yardage will depend on desired size. Choose cotton, silk, wool, linen, felt, etc. Allow at least 3-inch border all around for finishing

Thread for basting and for appliqué

Embroidery needle and very sharp-pointed scissors

Trace appliqué outline from the photograph. Enlarge tracing to any size by photostat. Trace photostat on a sheet of tracing paper. If necessary, tape several sheets of tracing paper to obtain the size you need.

Transfer design outline with dressmaker's carbon on one of the two fabrics and baste it to the other one. Baste several horizontal lines at 2-inch intervals to hold fabrics firmly together.

Cut out small areas at a time and stitch the cut edges with small blind stitches, folding back a bit of the fabric as you go. It is important to remember this small fold-back allowance when tracing the design outline. The fold-back allowance depends entirely on size of work and fabric used.

A small appliqué worked in thin cotton fabric would require about ⅛-inch fold-back, whereas wool or velvet would require at least ¼ inch. Felt does not need folding under and is a good choice for this type of appliqué.

To create the eye, slip a small piece of white fabric under eye opening, fasten it with a black cross-stitch (page 172) in center, and outline with large open buttonhole stitches (page 175).

Design outline may be worked in chain stitch (page 171) in contrasting color. When appliqué is completed, remove bastings, press, and mount as desired.

San Blas reverse appliqué.

DAHOMEY APPLIQUÉ

The Fon people of Abomey, capital city of Dahomey in Africa, developed the art of making appliqué cloth several hundred years ago. This cloth was used for military and religious banners, cult clothing, and state umbrellas and was displayed by people of rank and importance on ceremonial occasions.

This simple appliqué technique was done by cutting symbolic figures from brightly colored cloth and sewing them onto a backing of black, gold, or white cloth in such a way as to create a story.

This is similar in character to picture writing, and important chiefs and warriors memorialized their deeds on white umbrellas given them by the king. These have been compared to the heraldic banners of European nobility.

The making of appliqué cloth in Dahomey was and is the prerogative of men. In the past, members of these families enjoyed a high social position because of their close association with royal clients. The head of the family or chief was in charge of the guild that controlled the prices and the authenticity of traditional designs.

Today, a great deal of Dahomey appliqué is sold to tourists. Cloths are not as large nor is the appliqué as impressive, and the color range is wider. However, the symbolic figures are still cut from the original patterns, and the techniques are completely traditional.

INSTRUCTIONS

Materials

> Background cloth in gold, black, or white
> Cloth for appliqué shapes in colors indicated in Plate 27
> Cotton sewing thread or single strands of six-strand cotton embroidery floss
> Appropriate sharp needle
> Scissors, pins, tracing and transfer paper

All fabric is lightweight washable cotton cloth, and the actual size of the finished pieces is approximately 32 by 48 inches.

Enlarge to any size following instructions on pages 8–9, or do it freehand. Trace the largest shape outlines on the corresponding fabrics. Cut them out, allowing ¼ inch for folding under. Background fabric should be large enough to accommodate entire appliqué with not more than about 1 inch space allowance at the border. Press all fabrics.

Position the cutout shapes on the background fabric as indicated in the photograph and pin in place. Clip around curves and into corners *up to* but not *into* fold line. Baste all around, folding back margin with the needle as you go. If the appliqué is large, it is advisable to pin backing to a hard, smooth surface such as a table or floor to prevent it from shifting while the appliqué shapes are being pinned and basted. Remove all pins and stitch work in the hand.

Appliqué from Dahomey.
Courtesy African-
American Institute.

Dahomey appliqué is worked with simple blind or running stitches (page 170) in colors to match the appliqué shapes. The stitches are rather slapdash and not too fine. This adds to the primitive charm of the overall piece.

Cut, pin, baste, and stitch the smaller appliqué pieces. Be sure to stitch through all layers of fabric.

To finish, fold back margin all around. Trim edge with ribbon or a strip of fabric in any of the colors in the appliqué.

Attach hanging rings or slip a rod through the top seam. There is no need to line the appliqué.

Note: Make a Dahomey appliqué in fine fabrics such as velvet or silk and overembroider here and there with some shiny threads or couched gold trim. Let it hang as a tapestry or frame in a simple narrow frame.

Any of the symbolic shapes may be cut out singly and appliquéd on a rich black background to be used as a pillow top or small picture.

129

ISRAELI NEEDLEWORK

There is a new and exciting upsurge in contemporary needlework design in Israel, and many serious artists have adopted fabric and yarn techniques in their work with striking results.

A growing number of artists' colonies are supporting schools, workshops, and galleries in all media. The Artists' Village in Ein Hod is situated in the Carmel Mountains a few minutes' drive from Haifa. Founded by Marcel Janco, a Rumanian-born painter, Ein Hod is also the headquarters of the Mambush workshop in tapestry and stitchery.

The Meskit workshops, with locations in Jerusalem and Tel Aviv, have made great contributions in the field. Under the direction of Ruth Dayan, a thriving industry produces ethnic hand embroideries from vastly different cultures.

Bedouin women embroider traditional cross-stitch patterns in bright shimmering threads on black or white cotton dresses like the magnificent sample shown in Plate 29.

The couching of gold and silver threads as decorative borders on festival clothes is an old Yemenite technique. Such borders are embroidered on kaftans as well as Western dresses and are very popular with tourists. See page 134.

The "Exodus" Tapestry

In honor of the Bicentennial celebration of the United States, the America-Israel Cultural Foundation invited Kopel Gurwin, one of Israel's most prominent artists, to create an original tapestry entitled "Exodus" (Plate 28).

It is based on the historical fact that Benjamin Franklin, Thomas Jefferson, and John Adams once proposed that the theme of the Exodus be adapted for the seal of the United States of America. The legend on the seal reads: "Rebellion to tyrants is obedience to God." The intention was to compare the Pilgrims' crossing of the Atlantic to freedom in a new world to the Exodus of the Children of Israel from Egypt in ancient times.

This tapestry measures 72 by 72 inches and is worked entirely in felt appliqué on a background of dark green wool fabric. Felt is wonderful to work with, especially when color and configuration rather than texture are important in the overall design. Felt is not a woven fabric, it will not ravel, and it needs no folding under.

130

"Flowers." Tapestry, dark green felt appliqué on cream linen. Israel. Designed by Kopel Gurwin. Courtesy the America-Israel Cultural Foundation, New York.

The second tapestry, "Flowers" (above), is designed and worked by the same artist. It is also felt appliqué with a more restrained use of color and shape: a dark green, lacy cutout on cream-colored, handwoven linen with only a few colors for highlights. It measures 60 by 86 inches.

The artist has fastened all the appliqué pieces with evenly spaced, straight holding stitches. These stitches are not invisible, but because of their uniformity they seem to disappear into the background.

Note: Felt is not always available in a large variety of colors, but it may be dyed in the same manner as wool yarn. To obtain several closely related shades, mix a dark solution in a given color and dip the pieces of felt one at a time. Each

"Flowers" Tapestry

131

132   succeeding piece will come out a shade lighter than the previous one. The length of time required for each dipping will depend on the dye used, the thickness of the felt, and water temperature. Experiment with a few scraps before plunging valuable materials in a dye bath.

Felt becomes thicker and more durable when dipped in hot water. It also shrinks a lot. Cut felt pieces generously and cut out the appliqué shapes *after* the dyed pieces have been dried and pressed. To obtain clear, fresh pastel shades, always begin with white felt, which is readily available in yard goods stores. See general information on appliqué, page 14.

Bedouin Dress   The Bedouin dress in Plate 29 is nearly one hundred years old. It is fashioned in black homespun fabric woven on an 18-inch loom. The narrow strips of fabric are sewn together into a simple dress with narrow sleeves, wide skirt, and no collar. The front, back, and side panels, as well as parts of the sleeves, are embroidered with the brilliant colors typical of that part of the Middle East.

Detail of the Bedouin dress in Plate 29.

The entire dress is worked in long-legged cross-stitch. The threads are not counted accurately and are stitched "by eye." The cross-stitches are fairly even, or seem to be, and if they get out of line, they are compensated for with a shorter stitch now and then.

What pulls it all together are the lozenge or diamond geometric shapes and the stained glass colors set on a flat black background. The colors are red, magenta, gold, and peacock shades of blue and green. Extra brilliance is achieved with polished cottons or silk threads (see list of suppliers, page 178).

The pattern and colors are easy to duplicate from the color plate. Counted threads are more reliable, but if the fabric is dense and you have a good eye, try the Bedouin method.

This cross-stitch pattern is very attractive in decorative panels and borders on clothes and accessories. On white fabric the colored threads will appear more vivid if they are outlined in black.

Silver couching from Yemen is also easy to duplicate from the photographs (see below and page 134). Draw a swirling outline in chalk pencil directly on fabric, fasten to an embroidery frame (not a hoop), and guide the metallic cord around the outline, couching it closely with light embroidery floss. Work several borders side by side with rows of buttonhole (page 175) or herringbone stitches (page 173) in between in colored silk or rayon threads.

Detail of silver couching.

Silver couching from Yemen. Courtesy Mrs. Jessica Seiden.

TURKISH NEEDLEWORK

Turkish embroideries, once famous for their exquisite gold and silk work on sheer silk fabric, may be seen only in private collections or in museums around the world. A popular, inexpensive line of embroidered articles of clothing and accessories is still produced in Turkey for local and tourist consumption. Embroideries are a minor export item.

Vest

The silk vest on page 136 was worn at the turn of the century by men as part of a festival costume. It is an outstanding example of embroidery of that era. It is comparatively easy to duplicate by anyone with a little sewing and embroidery expertise.

INSTRUCTIONS

Materials

One commercial bolero pattern without gussets or darts
White silk or silklike fabric (yardage as recommended in pattern information)*
1 ounce of white embroidery silk (filoselle)
1 ounce of gold embroidery thread (Schurer metallic number 706)
Commercial gold lace to place all around as edging

The original vest is embroidered on white semisheer silk fabric with shiny white silk and fine gold metallic threads. The materials recommended above are the nearest you can buy on today's market.

Press the fabric and the pattern pieces. Use the back and the front pieces only. Do not use facing or pockets (if any).

Outline the back and two front parts on three separate rectangles of fabric. Use a fine-line acrylic marking pen and flip pattern to get a right and a left side.

Enlarge the embroidery pattern (page 137) by photostat and trace it on a sheet of tracing paper with a black marking pen of medium thickness. This will make the design visible on both sides of the tracing paper and therefore easier to trace as it is flipped over to the right or the left of the pattern piece.

*Note: Since each pattern part is outlined individually on a rectangle of fabric, you may need additional yardage. Purchase the pattern first, then measure the pattern parts, allowing a 6-inch margin around each rectangle, and estimate the amount of fabric needed.

Transfer design to fabric according to general instructions, pages 9–11 (do not use a hot-iron method on silk fabric). The embroidery pattern on the back of the vest is the same as on the two front pieces. Compensate the higher neckline in back with an extra flower motif.

Do not cut out the pattern pieces at this time. Fasten each rectangle of fabric with its individual pattern outline to an embroidery frame. Embroider flowers and paisley motifs with close satin stitch (page 170) and outline them with chain stitch (page 171) in white silk thread. Fill the large open flower centers with

Turkish bolero. The Metropolitan Museum of Art, Gift of Mrs. John Jay Whitehead, 1943.

closely couched gold thread (page 172). The original is worked in pulled-thread embroidery (see page 91) with fine flexible gold threads. Contemporary gold thread is too brittle to be used in pulled thread.

When the embroidery is completed, trim all tail ends and cut out the pattern parts, leaving a ½-inch margin all around. Fold back and slip stitch the margin. Edge each part with gold lace and assemble the vest by stitching the lace edge to edge at the shoulders and sides. The edging may be worked in needlemade or crochet lace, in which case you may need additional gold thread.

INDIAN NEEDLEWORK

The needlework of India along with other Eastern embroideries has for centuries excited the admiration of the world for the magnificence displayed in both materials and workmanship. No Western nation has ever attained the knowledge and management of color that Indian workmen displayed before the introduction of European dyes.

The embroidery was carried to such great intricacy and perfection of stitch and design composition that the pieces are nearly impossible to duplicate. We can only admire the skill and unlimited patience that went into the execution of each fraction of an inch of space covered with small intricate stitches in gold and silk threads.

Today, much of Indian embroidery is exported. The quality of workmanship, design, and color placement does not begin to approach the splendor of antiquity, but there is a constant effort to improve all handcrafted items. Some contemporary silk embroideries are truly remarkable.

Indian Camis   I would like to share with you the visual pleasure of an antique embroidery from India. It is a *camis* or kaftan that was fashionable in the late part of the eighteenth and early nineteenth centuries (Plate 30). Each little circle, oval, and square design unit is made up of from one to four shisha chips each, roughly the size of a small sequin.

Shisha work is embroidery incorporating bits of mirror or mica fastened with a circle of holding stitches (see stitch detail, page 140). The shisha is carefully outlined with fine buttonhole holding stitches, some in circlets and others with the stitches foreshortened in three corners to create a triangle.

On this *camis*, the shisha chips are outlined, in addition to the basic holding stitch, with rows of chain and backstitches worked with perfect regularity and beautifully controlled color scheme.

Contemporary shisha work is done with Mylar (see page 140) or cardboard-backed aluminum foil, and the shapes are fairly large. The effect is still attractive when used judiciously. However, the shisha in the antique *camis* are real mirror chips, and the embroidery must have been done by the tiniest hands imaginable.

Detail of Indian *camis*, Plate 30. The Metropolitan Museum of Art. Gift of Mr. and Mrs. Clarence S. Stein, 1962.

Girls were trained from early childhood to sit for hours at the embroidery frames, and it took years to perfect their skill. So don't expect to be able to duplicate the entire *camis*.

The diagram above shows the outline of the medallion at the base of the pattern, and a black-and-white detail of the embroidery is on page 139. These plus the stitch details following should prove helpful in design construction.

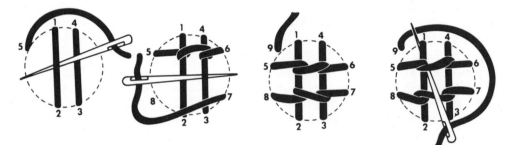

Shisha stitch. Original shisha work is done with mirror chips. However, it is much easier to use Mylar, a mirrorlike aluminum with fabric backing. It is available in art supply stores and may be cut with scissors. If Mylar is not available, use heavy-duty aluminum foil, shiny side out, over lightweight cardboard or extra-large silver sequins. Cut Mylar or foil into circles. Place circle on fabric and work two sets of parallel stitch lines like a tic-tac-toe frame. Intertwine the second pair of stitches, as indicated in the diagram. Bring needle out on the outer outline and work a tight buttonhole stitch all around. Work through the center square formed by the parallel stitch lines as your top line. (See buttonhole stitch, page 175.) Shape the center square into a circle by adjusting the stitches as you work around the Mylar circle. For best results, the buttonhole circle should not be less than one-third the width of the Mylar.

The kaftan is decorated almost entirely with shisha work. Practice shisha stitch on large circles at first, then make them progressively smaller. Use it to decorate clothing, pillows, and so on.

Note: This design can be adapted to cross-stitch or crewel and embellished with beads or sequins. Work up a small sample first before attempting a large project, and remember that this is very elaborate embroidery and a little goes a long way.

140

This is not tambour work, which is generally associated with chain stitch in India. Tambour is not really needlework, since it is made with a crochetlike tool and not a threaded needle. It is also worked while the piece is stretched on a frame.

This rug, shown in Plate 31, is worked in the hand in chain stitch, and the effect is exactly the same as tambour. The actual size including border is 48 by 72 inches. If fabric width permits, the rug may be enlarged a little, but it should always be worked in one piece. Any seams would be visible and would detract from the design.

INSTRUCTIONS

Materials

2¼ yards of heavy-duty embroidery linen, 54 inches wide
2¼ yards of burlap for lining in the same width
Three-ply yarn in navy, purple, bright green, light and dark turquoise, and sand beige. Work with two plies*
Crewel needle, number 18
Basting thread (bright, highly visible color)
Tracing and transfer paper
Pencil, pins, scissors

Edge cut sides of linen with machine stitching and outline the design border with a heavy chalk line. Study Plate 31 carefully. There is a closeup detail as well as a diagram on pages 142–143. Notice that the basic shape of the predominant pattern is similar to a lemon.

There are three large "lemons" in one row and two smaller ones plus two halves in the second row. They alternate.

Enlarge diagram following instructions on pages 8–9. The actual dimension of the large lemon pattern is 15 by 20 inches high. Use it as a repeat pattern and transfer it, beginning at center top. (See general transfer directions on pages 9–11.)

The pattern may be simplified a little by omitting some of the detail. Work chain stitches (page 171) in close rows, following design outlines. Stitches should be of medium size and as even as possible. Rows of stitches must fit comfortably and cover the linen fabric without crowding.

Avoid pulling thread and keep an even tension. Study the black-and-white detail and try to duplicate the direction of the chain stitch lines. Work one color at a time.

When rug is finished, place it on a flat surface, right side up, and press over a damp cloth. Press burlap lining. (Lining may be assembled for narrower pieces if necessary.)

Miter corners as shown on page 43 on both the worked linen and lining. Pin both back to back. Check margins for evenness and adjust pins as needed. Burlap lining should be slightly shorter than the linen and should not show above the embroidery.

Baste both fabrics and remove pins. Finish with small, close stitches worked on the lining side and remove bastings.

Note: If the rug is to be used as a wall hanging, finish top and sides only. Leave bottom edge open and hem each fabric individually on the wrong side.

*It is not possible to give exact amount of yarn needed to complete this rug. It is suggested, therefore, that you purchase 3 ounces in each color, work up an area of the design, and see how far it takes you. Estimate balance by simple multiplication.

Detail of chain stitch rug, Plate 31.

BURMESE NEEDLEWORK

Burmese Wall Hanging

The overall size of the antique wall hanging from Burma is 6 by 12 feet. It is a nineteenth-century folk craft appliqué depicting a battle scene between the Thais and the Burmese (Plate 32).

Most wall hangings of this size are displayed in temples, palaces, and museums. They are very impressive and look extremely complicated. This one is a comparatively simple appliqué with stylized figures and overembroidery with couching and sequins. If couching is not your favorite technique, use a heavier thread and work it in chain stitch.

If you are going to try your hand at a really large project, you might want to practice on a small section first. For this reason I have reproduced here a part of the appliqué shown opposite and in outline on pages 146–147.

INSTRUCTIONS

Enlarge to 18 by 13½ inches according to general instructions on pages 8–9. Make two tracings of the design. Select appliqué fabrics and transfer the outlines onto the background. Cut out all the figures from the second tracing as you would paper cutouts and baste them to the appliqué fabric. Cut fabric around paper patterns leaving a ¼-inch margin all around. Clip into corners and around curves to facilitate fold-back.

Do not remove papers. Pin each appliqué piece to its own outline on the background. Baste carefully and remove pins. Check embroidery outline on photograph and work it with either couching or chain stitch through paper and fabric. For best results use a frame.

Indicate sequin placement by piercing paper pattern with a fine-point marking pen. As you apply the dot, pierce the paper and it will leave a small impression on the fabric. Remove all papers and bastings and sew sequins where indicated.

If your background fabric is lightweight, baste a square of muslin on the reverse side of appliqué and sew the sequins through all thicknesses of fabric.

The small stylized bird is a repeat pattern for the border, but it will make an attractive picture by itself.

You can duplicate the large appliqué, or parts of it, using the same method. When you work with many small figures in appliqué, it is helpful to divide the

Detail of Burmese hanging, Plate 32.

work into several sections with chalk lines. Identify each section with a letter or a number. Cross-reference the paper patterns for the figures and keep them in separate boxes.

Appliqué one area at a time; and once the figures are placed, proceed to over-embroider at leisure. A wall hanging this size should take approximately one year to finish—about as long as it takes to needlepoint a small rug. However, the appliqué would not be nearly as expensive and will certainly be more original.

145

Heavier lines are couching

Border motif (one-quarter)
Heavier lines are couching

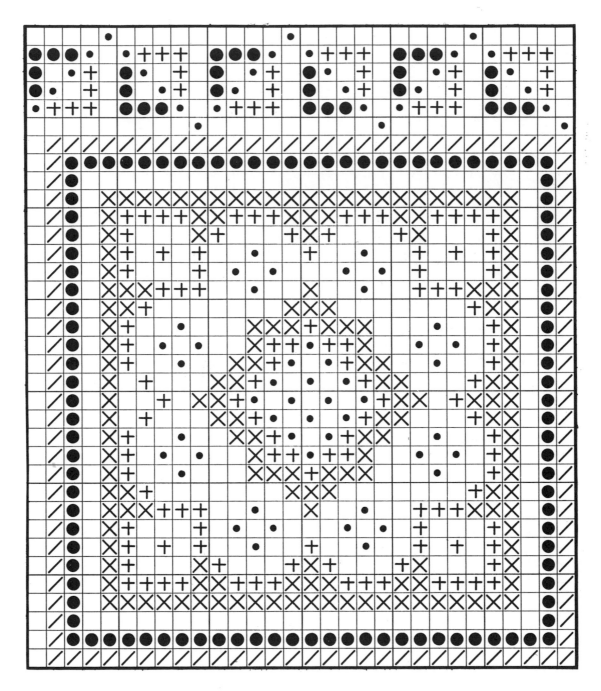

□ Black

● Green

/ Pink

• White

✕ Light green

+ Magenta

CAMBODIAN NEEDLEWORK

Cambodian needlework is not as well known internationally as that from other Asian countries, but it does have the same fine workmanship and delicate color balance.

The sample shown in Plate 33 is a contemporary pillow top worked in a combination of cross-stitch and appliqué on black cotton fabric with cotton and silk threads. **Pillow Top**

A square of forty-count cotton (forty strands to the inch) was embroidered in the center with twelve rectangle patterns. The patterns are identical; only the colors differ. Plate 34 is an enlargement of this pattern worked on number 10 mesh canvas with wool yarns and white rayon as highlight. The enlargement is shown as a detail to clarify design construction.

The graph opposite shows cross-stitch placement and color key. In the actual needlework the crosses are worked in rectangular shapes, over two square mesh at top and bottom and over one square mesh at the sides. This allows for an additional horizontal crossover line. It resembles an unfinished Smyrna cross. The design may be altered by stitching full Smyrna crosses, in which case the patterns will be square instead of rectangular.

The borders are all worked in appliqué strips in gold, green, red, and white, mitered and stitched to the black background. The white border is cut away to reveal the black, and the widest red borders are overstitched with long-legged cross-stitches (page 173) held down with small white stitches at the crossover points.

It is a very interesting piece of work, and it could be made into a large wall hanging. Use number 5 mesh canvas and rug yarn with heavy rayon threads. Make as many squares as you wish. Work the appliqué border separately in colorful wools or velvets and attach to canvas.

CHINESE NEEDLEWORK

The small nineteenth-century Chinese embroidery shown in Plate 35 is a perfect example of the exquisite workmanship and special care given to minutest detail. Since design and choice of color are always matters of personal taste, I cannot in all fairness commit myself to a specific geographical area and pinpoint it as the one producing the most beautiful designs.

I can, however, say without hesitation that Chinese embroidery ranks among the very finest in the world in quality and delicacy of workmanship. Even today, when hand embroidery is an export business and production speed is important, the quality remains unchanged.

The embroidery in Plate 36 is worked in silk threads on a red silk background. The stitches are long and short, couched, and there is a great deal of laid work couched down with some really fancy work. There is also a charming trellis in three shades of blue, white, and red intertwined stitches. The actual size of this embroidery is 21 by 34 inches, but it can be made larger.

Enlarge diagram (opposite) and transfer it to the silk background with dressmaker's carbon paper. Allow enough margin on fabric to drape over an embroidery frame. The design outline should not come right up to the edge of the frame but should be about 3 inches inside the frame's outline.

If you have never worked this type of embroidery, I recommend a few private lessons with a good instructor. You should then have a better-than-average understanding of the stitchery technique involved. (Stitch techniques are described on pages 171, 172, and 174.)

To make the faces, trace the outline of each face on a piece of white felt. Cut out the shapes and make sure that they fit perfectly inside the corresponding outline on the fabric ground. Cover them completely with pale cream embroidery silk floss as in laid work, long stitches covering the entire length of the face from hat line to below neckline. Work slowly and carefully, following contour of face. Trace the facial features on small squares of thin tracing paper. Place paper squares on the corresponding figures in such a way as to position the facial expression over the laid silk. Pin the paper outside the facial contour and embroider the face through paper, silk, felt, and backing. The entire embroidery should be worked on a frame.

Use fine single strands of silk or cotton embroidery floss. Work eyes, mouth, and nose outlines. Pull the stitches tight to bring out the padding. Remove the paper gently. Use the back of the needle to help it along.

Finish the face by filling in the color of eyes and mouth. Facial contours may be outlined with cream-colored silk.

Repeat with the other faces. Embroider the hats, robes, and then the long moustache. I suggest that you work a few faces on a practice cloth before doing them on the real thing.

The finished embroidery is backed and framed with antique silk.

Note: The Chinese embroiderers were masters of their craft and were able to embroider and virtually sculpt padded laid work without the aid of tracing papers. However, I have found my method helpful to those who cannot copy facial features without some tracing outline.

Chinese Coat   The pattern takes 1¾ yards of 36-inch or 45-inch fabric for medium size.

INSTRUCTIONS

1. Enlarge pattern according to general directions.
2. Lay out fabric folded in half lengthwise.
3. Pin pattern to fabric on the lengthwise grain and cut out all parts. You should have two coat front pieces and two coat back pieces. Unpin pattern.
4. Stitch the backs together on the center back seam taking ½-inch seam allowance. Press seam open.
5. Stitch the fronts to the back at the shoulder, matching sleeve edges and front neck edge to back neck point. Press seams open.

Chinese silk ceremonial coat.
The Metropolitan Museum of Art,
Bequest of William Christian
Paul, 1930.

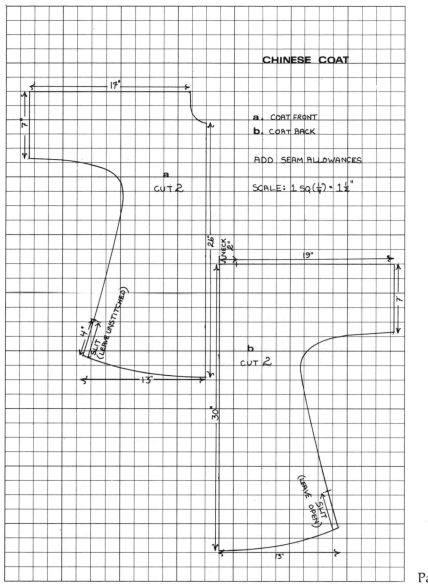

CHINESE COAT

17"

a. COAT FRONT
b. COAT BACK

ADD SEAM ALLOWANCES

SCALE: 1 SQ ($\frac{1}{4}$") = 1$\frac{1}{2}$"

a
CUT 2

26"

NECK 2"

19"

SLIT
(LEAVE UNSTITCHED)

4"

b
CUT 2

13"

30"

SLIT
(LEAVE OPEN)

13"

Pattern by Carol Peretz.

6. Stitch the front parts to the back along the underarm seams and down the sides up to 4 inches from hemline. Clip around curves and press seams flat.

7. Make a second identical coat in a different fabric and use it as a lining. Slip outer coat over the lining. Align them carefully. Now fold back all raw edges ½ inch around sleeves, collar, side slits, bottom, and front opening on the outer coat. Baste all around. On the inside of the coat, fold the lining ¾ inch the same way and pin it fold to fold all around. Check carefully to see that the lining lies smooth and even and is tucked ¼ inch inside the outer fabric. Adjust pins if necessary and baste. Finish with fine herringbone (page 173) or blind stitches. Press coat and fasten with hooks and eyes or "frogs."

153

Chinese robe. The Metropolitan Museum of Art, Rogers Fund, 1942.

Chinese Robe   The robe requires 5 yards of 36- or 45-inch fabric for medium size.

INSTRUCTIONS

1. Enlarge pattern according to general directions (see pages 8–9).
2. Lay fabric flat. Pin pattern pieces to the fabric on the lengthwise grain. Place neckband and ties on the true bias.

    Cut: 2 back pieces
    1 left front
    1 right front
    1 front overlap
    2 neckbands
    4 bias ties

    Unpin pattern pieces.
3. Stitch center back seam taking up ½-inch seam allowance. Press seam open.
4. Stitch front overlap pieces to left front on long edge. Press seam open.
5. Stitch back to front along shoulder seams. Press seam.
6. Stitch underarm seams and down the side up to seam opening. Trim seam allowance under the arm curve and press seams open.
7. Stitch the two neckbands together, wrong sides in. Turn right side out and press.

154

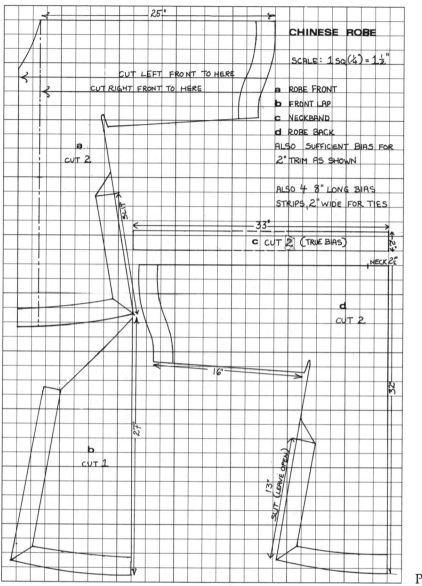

Within the figure:

CHINESE ROBE

SCALE: 1 SQ ($\frac{1}{4}$) = 1$\frac{1}{2}$"

25"

CUT LEFT FRONT TO HERE
CUT RIGHT FRONT TO HERE

a ROBE FRONT
b FRONT LAP
c NECKBAND
d ROBE BACK
ALSO SUFFICIENT BIAS FOR
2" TRIM AS SHOWN

ALSO 4 8" LONG BIAS
STRIPS, 2" WIDE FOR TIES

a
CUT 2

SLIT

33"

c CUT 2 (TRUE BIAS)

2"

NECK 2$\frac{1}{2}$"

d
CUT 2

16"

32"

27"

b
CUT 1

13" SLIT (LEAVE OPEN)

Pattern by Carol Peretz.

8. Baste the neckband to the robe along the neck edge, beginning at the front overlap and continuing around the back and down the right front edge. Try on to see if it lies smooth. Stitch through one thickness only and remove basting. Now, turn the other edge under ½ inch and slip stitch by hand.

9. Place sleeve trim on top of the fabric at sleeve edge. Fold in both edges and slip stitch by hand.

10. Make a second robe in lining fabric, minus the bias trim. Stitch lining by hand, folding it in a little more so that it does not show.

11. Fold the 2-inch-wide bias strips in half lengthwise and stitch, taking up ½-inch seam allowance to make ½-inch tubing. Turn right side out and stitch in place as shown in photograph as fasteners, or use hooks.

155

Chinese Jacket   The rare embroidered jacket shown in Plate 36 was made of blue wool broadcloth rather than silk. One diagram of a flower detail is shown below. The pattern is not reproduced here but I hope it serves as a source of inspiration for something truly beautiful.

Chinese embroidered shawls have been prized in Spain for over a century and have become so identified with Spanish fashion that their oriental origin has been almost forgotten and often denied.

The earliest shawls imported from the Orient were scarves from India. These were soon followed by the famous shawls from Kashmir, also rectangular in shape, which derived their name from the Persian word *chal*.

As the crinoline fashion developed, square shawls made their first appearance folded in half into a triangle. Shawls of all kinds became very popular.

The scarves and shawls from India were handwoven in wool and nearly always had dark backgrounds. The Chinese shawls, in light silk and fine embroidery in splendid colors, must have been a striking change in fashion.

Tradition has it that the first silk shawls, or *mantones* as they were known in Spain, were introduced into southern Spain by a merchant from Manila, and it was assumed that they were made in the Philippines. This was not the case. The port of Manila was chiefly a trade center for goods exported to the Western world when trade with China was uncertain for political reasons.

The *mantones de Manila* were made in China. Whatever their source of origin, they were immediately adopted by Spanish ladies and retained their popularity for nearly one hundred years.

Chinese shawls were first introduced in Europe around 1830. They were quite simple, with narrow embroidered borders in monotones and no center motif. The fringes were rather short and fine, and the workmanship was superlative.

As demand for these shawls increased, so did the opulent needlework. Borders became wider, and center motifs extended almost to the borders. By the middle of the nineteenth century the shawls were quite large, with elaborate embroidery patterns covering the silk background. The fringes reached a length of 16 inches.

Shawls were unknown in China as an article of fashion and were produced strictly for export. Since most of them were shipped to Europe, the patterns and colors were influenced by European preferences. However, the meticulous Chinese method of workmanship remained unchanged, and no one else in the world has been able to duplicate it.

Embroidered shawls enjoyed a brief popularity in several European countries; for a time, some beautiful creations were embroidered in Italy, France, Greece, and even Spain.

The elegant *mantones de Manila* are no longer manufactured. Those that remained were rapidly absorbed into museums and private collections. It is still possible to buy a beauty, but authentic old Chinese embroideries are rare and quite expensive.

Illustrated are three embroidered silk shawls from different parts of the world. Plate 37 and Plate 38 show shawls from China, and Plate 39 shows one from Italy. All three are relatively easy to reproduce with the aid of the diagrams and a little needlework expertise.

INSTRUCTIONS

To duplicate any of the shawls you will need a 48-inch square of very fine silk fabric, some silk embroidery floss in the colors indicated in the color plates, a sharp embroidery needle, and a small embroidery hoop.

Select fabric carefully. Drape it around your shoulders to see how it hangs. It should feel soft and luxurious and be of a medium weight necessary to support the embroidery.

158   Draw a 48-inch square on a large, flat surface. Press the silk and place it within this square. Clip and adjust fabric so that it fits inside the outline. Fold the edges over twice to form a ¼-inch margin all around. Pin and baste with small stitches.

Press fabric again if necessary and transfer the enlarged pattern as described in the general instructions on pages 9–11. The diagram outlines for shawls are given in quarter patterns. Enlarge them to one-quarter of the overall size of the shawl and assemble the entire pattern on a 48-inch square of tracing paper. Use this total pattern to transfer design.

COLOR KEY
1 = Light green
2 = Mauve
3 = Pink
See Plate 37

Center motif

If silk fabric is less than 48 inches wide, bear this in mind when enlarging pattern diagram. There should be a border allowance of about 2 inches between embroidery and fringe.

Place silk with a small portion of the design transfer on an embroidery hoop (a size you find comfortable to handle), and stretch it gently until the surface is firm and smooth but not distorted. Work the stems with stem stitch (page 170) and the flowers and leaves with satin stitch (page 170) to cover design outlines.

The three shawls are not difficult to embroider, and they are worked with two or three shades that are easy to identify from the color plate. Since all these shawls are old, it is not possible to match colors exactly, but I do suggest the use of soft shades.

Use short strands of silk and keep the wrong side of the work neat and free of tail ends. To do this, catch the thread on the wrong side as you begin, and tack it once over a thread or two of the fabric. Leave a tail end of about 1 inch, which you fold back with your finger as you work the first few stitches over and under to cover it. When the embroidery thread has to be ended off, again turn work over on the wrong side, take a tiny tack into the stitches, and slide the rest of the tail under them. Remove needle and clip any bit of thread that shows. The tiny tacks are important when working with silk thread, because it tends to slip out.

Finish all the embroidery inside the hoop and move it along until the entire shawl is finished. Dry clean before fringing to remove all transfer marks.

159

**One-quarter pattern
See Plate 38**

162

Fringes are a matter of personal taste. If you have the time and the expertise, do a macramé fringe—not too elaborate, since it must be remembered that the fringe is only an extension of the shawl fabric and must not overpower the embroidery.

The most elegant shawls have fringes that match the fabric and not the embroidery, so bear this in mind when selecting a silk fabric other than black. Fringes should be at least 6 inches long.

To estimate the amount of silk thread needed for fringes, take about 50 yards of thread and work up some fringe in the length and type you like best. If it covers, say, 10 inches and the four sides of the shawl measure a total of 180 inches all around, then 180 divided by 10 is 18, and 18 times 50 is 900 yards. Buy a little extra to be sure, and use a twisted silk thread that falls smoothly and does not curl.

Trim fringes for a clean, even edge.

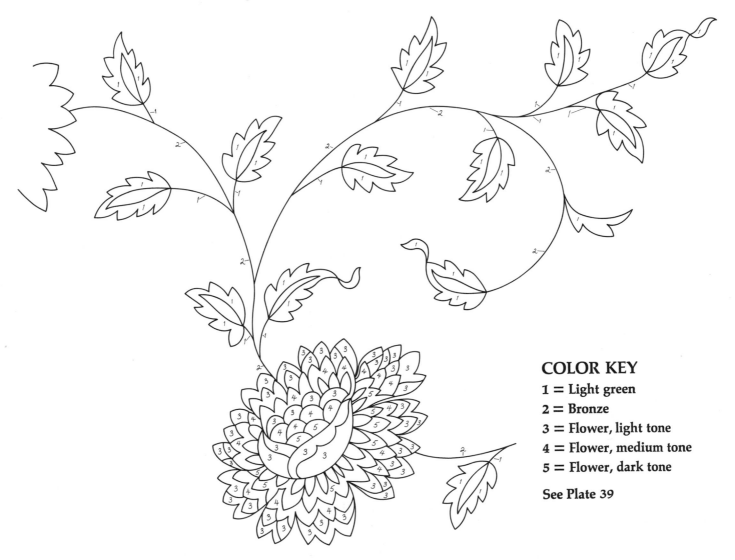

COLOR KEY

1 = Light green

2 = Bronze

3 = Flower, light tone

4 = Flower, medium tone

5 = Flower, dark tone

See Plate 39

JAPANESE NEEDLEWORK

Like most oriental needlework, that of Japan is extremely fine and worked with the greatest skill. The stitches are mostly small and flat, such as satin or the long and short, and the emphasis is on design projection.

Some Japanese embroideries look like fine paintings, and only on close scrutiny is it evident that the little fine lines are not pen-and-ink strokes but thousands of little stitches worked in silk with infinite care.

Obviously work like this takes years of practice and superior artistic talent. It is impossible to duplicate with a few diagrams. However, Japanese designs are light and graceful and may be adapted to almost any fabric and stitchery.

Obi

I selected two nineteenth-century *obi* with repeat all-over patterns that may be used singly with excellent results (see Plate 40). The *obi* is a long sash used as a tie belt on a woman's kimono and is generally woven or embroidered in exquisite designs.

The cranes in flight are typically Japanese and very popular in ornamental embroidery. The *obi* is needlewoven in a pattern that resembles bargello brick stitch. If you examine the diagram outline on page 164 you will see that it may be easily adapted to the half cross-stitch, either continental or basketweave.

The fans are also handwoven and may be adapted to stitchery in much the same manner as the cranes. However, I think it would translate best into a large appliqué work. Think in terms of beautiful one-of-a-kind or antique fabrics cut into fan shapes and worked in appliqué on a background of embossed silk brocade or a lush satin. Make a marvelous bed cover or wall hanging or trim a kimono.

Japanese Kimono   The literal meaning of the word *kimono* in its original sense is "clothing." Kimono is associated exclusively with the unique national costume that instantly identifies Japan around the world. Kimono includes the traditional male costume, but in contemporary Japan it is the exception rather than the rule for a man to wear a kimono ensemble.

Even for girls and women the kimono has long since ceased to be everyday wear. It is too complex and constricting a fashion for the active life of modern Japan. Yet, it remains unchanged as the high-fashion garment for purely Japanese occasions such as festival celebrations, weddings, and funerals.

When the kimono is worn in Japan, certain long-established traditions are still followed such as fabric selection, color, style, and the special tying of the *obi* (sash). The manufacture of ready-made garments and special fabrics for kimonos is a flourishing business in Japan but virtually nonexistent in the Western world. (The few Western stores that carry Japanese kimonos offer a limited variety in their better-quality line, and the cheaper stock is not worth mentioning.)

The Japanese kimono is one of the most charming and feminine articles of clothing and may be reproduced quite easily from the dressmaker's pattern on page 169. Choose an attractive medium-weight fabric and overembroider it.

It is not necessary to use much embroidery, because a little goes a long way. Select a part of the print you wish to highlight. Outline some areas with embroidery and fill in others. Use simple stitches such as chain, stem, or couching, and work with silk or polished cotton threads.

The total effect should be light and airy, and you should remember to repeat the embroidery each time there is a print repeat.

Examine the sleeve detail opposite. It is a *furisode*, or long sleeve, decorated with cranes, flowers, and foliage. The heads and wing tips of the cranes are embroidered with a few perfect stitches in white silk thread, only enough to create a little highlight. The rest of the design is painted and stenciled.

Plates 41 and 42 show antique kimonos from the world-famous Kanebo Collection. Both are splendid examples of blends in compatible techniques.

The *kosode,* "small sleeves," is a kimono with narrow hand openings at the end of the sleeves.

The *kosode* in green figured satin (*inzu*) has a surface decoration of maple leaves applied with *somenuki* dyeing. (This is a starch resist that is used over selected patterns to protect them when the fabric is dyed.) Some of the maple leaves were embroidered with a variety of stitches in rust-colored silk and gold and some were left plain.

The magnificent *kosode* with bold large-scale designs is an excellent example of the style that originated in the Kambun era, 1661–1673, after the fires that destroyed the wardrobes of much of Edo (Tokyo) in 1657 and Kyoto in 1661.

The large chrysanthemums, snowflake ring, and light vertical stripes are rendered in tie-dye. The dark stripes and areas in the main design are embroidered with a variety of blossoms and symbols of good fortune and wealth (*takarazukushi*).

You may not be able to duplicate these exactly, but I hope they may serve as a source of inspiration.

The traditional Japanese kimono is cut without shoulder seams. It is made with uncut lengths of fabric from the toes across the shoulders and down to the heels. The body of the kimono and the two sleeves compose the two principal parts of the pattern plus the neckband and side ties.

Sleeve detail of a Japanese kimono. The Metropolitan Museum of Art, Gift of Mrs. Ray C. Kramer, 1958.

168   Each panel is individually lined and finished. It is then sewn together along the seams by hand. The kimono is taken apart for cleaning and repair and sewn together again.

The kimono pattern has been modified to include shoulder seams for ease of handling, cutting, and construction. It is sewn together permanently and may be cleaned by conventional methods.

INSTRUCTIONS

The pattern opposite is for medium size. Each square equals 3 inches. For a smaller size, trim 1/2 inch off side seams on panels A and B. For a larger size add 1/2 inch to these seams.

Materials for full-length kimono
    4¼ yards of fabric, 45 inches wide
    4¼ yards of fabric for lining, 45 inches wide
    Sewing thread
    Embroidery threads as needed
    Appropriate needles
    Dressmaker's paper for drafting pattern

Enlarge pattern on special dressmaker's drafting paper, using a gauge of 1 square = 3 square inches. Cut the pattern parts and embroider or overembroider print. Check embroidery for loose threads and unfinished pieces, press, and assemble kimono as follows:

1. Stitch front overlap C to front B along seam edge.
2. Stitch front B to back A at shoulder seam, armhole to neck point.
3. Stitch two sleeve pieces E together along shoulder seam. Repeat with the other two pieces.
4. Stitch kimono A/B to sleeves E at the armhole seam.
5. Stitch side seams A/B from armhole to hemline.
6. Stitch sleeve starting at wrist opening and around to the armhole point.
7. Stitch neckband D along the edge A/B/C matching center back point. Fold the other edge of neckband over the stitched edge and slip stitch by hand with invisible stitches inside the kimono.

Press seams flat. Slip lining inside kimono wrong side to wrong side. Baste together at side seams, wrist openings, and neckband.

Adjust hemline and pin in place. Stitch lining to outer fabric by hand. Work with tiny, even stitches, keeping the lining slightly below the fabric edge so that it will not be visible on the right side.

Don't sew the fabrics together at hemline. Fold each only once against itself and stitch separately with a light herringbone hemstitch. Add inside ties as needed.

A sash or belt should be made separately in a contrasting fabric or ribbon. The simplest is fairly narrow and measures about 72 inches in length. It is sometimes possible to purchase a lovely *obi* in stores that handle oriental imports, but do this only if you know how to tie it.

The kimono pattern may be adjusted to fingertip length to make a *happi* coat to be worn over slacks.

Note: Although this pattern was adapted from an authentic Japanese kimono, it is described as an elegant leisure dress for Western wear. It is not the intention of the author to present the kimono as it is worn and draped in Japan.

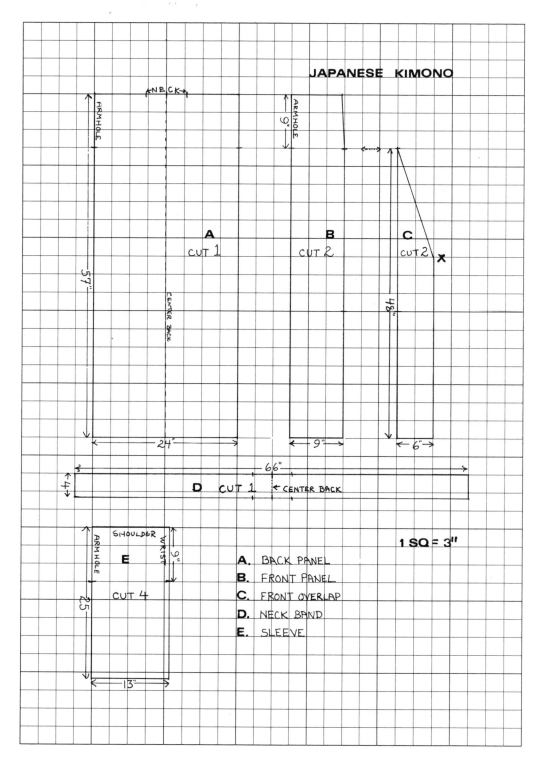

JAPANESE KIMONO

A. BACK PANEL
B. FRONT PANEL
C. FRONT OVERLAP
D. NECK BAND
E. SLEEVE

1 SQ = 3"

Pattern by Carol Peretz.

STITCH DETAILS

Running stitch Bring needle over and under the fabric to create a row of evenly spaced stitches on both the surface and the underside. The top stitches may be a different size from those on the underside.

This is the simplest of needlework. It is used as a basting stitch as well as in decorative outlines. A smaller, tighter version is the quilting stitch.

Double running stitch is achieved when, on the return row, the running stitch is worked in reverse, covering all the spaces. The effect is that of a backstitch except that both sides of the work look the same. Work from right to left.

Backstitch Work from right to left along a design outline. Begin a stitch length away from the end, pull out the threaded needle, go back into the end point, and in a continuous motion bring the needle out in front of the point of exit and one stitch length away. Repeat. Stitches should be very even and the needle must always be placed into the point of exit of the preceding stitch.

Stem stitch Work from left to right along the design outline. Stitches are slightly slanted and of equal size. Practice the stem stitch on a variety of drawn outlines and learn to curve it gracefully. It is very useful in fine-line stitchery.

The pen-and-ink sketch on page 48 was worked in the stem stitch rather than in the quilting stitch. The Finnish embroideries (pages 86 and 88) are worked in a slight variation of the stem. The surface stitches are quite long and the needle catches only a small bit of the fabric on the underside.

Satin stitch A very popular embroidery stitch that may be worked straight or slanted. Stitches should be smooth with an even outline and should cover an area completely. If fabric shows in spots, add another stitch or two. Satin stitch requires practice.

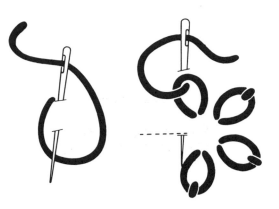

Chain stitch Work from left to right or top to bottom. Bring needle out and loop thread under its point. Pull needle gently to form a rounded loop stitch. Repeat by inserting needle in the same spot where the thread came out inside the previous loop.

Chain stitch may be used as outline where a bolder, heavier line is desired. It may also be used as fill; begin in the center and work in pinwheel fashion, or work several rows side by side and in the same direction.

Practice chain stitch if you are not familiar with it since it looks best when the loops are rounded and very even.

Lazy daisy A decorative stitch derived from the chain stitch. Each loop is placed individually around a small imaginary circle to form a daisy with five or six petals. First draw a small circle, and then add five or six lines around it like the spokes of a wheel.

Practice on this diagram until you learn to make the stitches freehand.

Open chain stitch A variation of the basic chain stitch. Work the same way as chain stitch but insert the needle to the right of the loop and bring it out to the left of the next loop. Do not pull too tight. The width of the chain can be varied. Some of the flower outlines on the Indian kaftan (see page 139) are worked in open chain stitch.

Long and short stitch A variation of satin stitch for areas too large to be covered with one long stitch. The long and short stitches do not have to be of equal length. Since several rows of stitches appear within one shape, they are very useful for shading. These stitches don't have to face in the same direction on one piece of needlework but are meant to conform to the individual shapes within it.

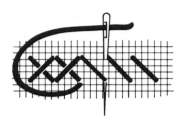

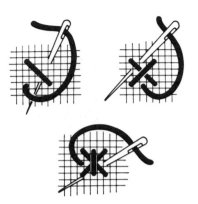

Cross-stitch Always worked on counted-thread fabric or canvas mesh. Two slanted stitches of equal length cross each other. The stitches may be worked from right to left or top to bottom one at a time; or work a line of half crosses and finish the other half on the return row, as indicated in the diagram. The top stitches must always slant in the same direction on a given work.

Double cross-stitch A textured bump stitch that begins as a conventional cross-stitch with an additional vertical and horizontal stitch added. The basic slanted stitches should be worked over an even number of fabric strands in order to create a center point for the last two stitches. The double cross-stitches are worked individually and the last stitch must always point in the same direction.

Couching Place a heavy thread along the design outline and "tie" it down with small stitches at regular intervals in a finer thread. The heavy thread is inserted through the fabric with another needle. If it is too heavy, or if it is metallic cord, use an embroidery stiletto to punch a hole in the fabric at the beginning and at the end of the couching outline. I might add that a stiletto does not break the fabric; it separates the fabric threads to accommodate the heavier thread. It is not necessary to knot or fasten the heavy guide thread in couching since it is kept in place by the small stitches. When couching stitches are slanted, they are referred to as Rumanian couching. Always work them in the same direction and keep them equidistant.

Overcast stitch A variation of the couching stitch where the small stitches are worked very close together and cover the guide thread completely. Work from left to right.

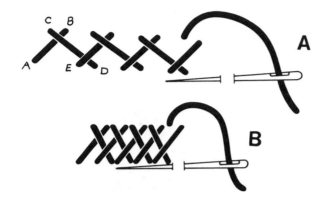

Herringbone stitch A type of cross-stitch that is always worked from left to right. An excellent and versatile border stitch, it may be worked in any length or width. Keep the spaces between stitches as even as possible. Practice on counted thread.

Cambodian long-legged herringbone An interesting variation on the herringbone stitch as worked around the border of the Cambodian needlework (see page 150). The herringbone legs are extra-long and are held in place at the cross-points with four little stitches worked individually to form a diamond.

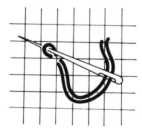

Eyelet overcast Work a running stitch around a circle. Punch a hole in the center of the circle with a stiletto or the points of embroidery scissors. Push back the ragged edge of the fabric and overcast with close stitches over the fabric edge and running stitch. For larger eyelet holes, slit the fabric in the center crosswise, push the cut edges to the underside, and work the overcast stitch. Trim any ragged edges on the wrong side of the work.

Slip knot This is very useful when working on open mesh and a minimum of tail ends is desirable. Begin by working with a thinner thread doubled over. Thread needle through double thickness and leave the loop at the far end. Bring threaded needle under the crossover point of two mesh threads and pull until only the loop is visible in the corner. Bring needle around and slip through the loop. Pull tightly.

Laid work When a design area is to be filled with extra-long stitches, the over-and-under motion of the satin stitch becomes impractical. Instead, the threads are laid on the surface of the fabric. Come up at 1, bring thread across to 2, then from 3 to 4, and so on. Leave just enough space between threads to accommodate one single thread on the return row, as indicated in the diagram. It is possible to make the stitches close enough to cover in one row, but I prefer this method, especially when the stitches are very long or the fabric is lightweight. Laid work must be placed on a stretcher or a hoop. If the design area is of an irregular shape, place your first thread across its widest part and work the rest parallel to it above and below. Long stitches should be held down and various stitches may be used for this. If the laid threads are silk and the overembroidery is gold or silver or contrasting silk colors, the effect is elegant.

The small Chinese wall hanging (Plate 35) utilizes laid work in the robes and in some of the background figures. The laid work is embroidered with gold couching and backstitches.

The Guatemalan altar cloth (Plate 26) is worked almost entirely in satin stitch with the exception of the large center rows in bright red. These are not overembroidered but are covered with two rows of laid stitches worked closely.

Seeding or speckling A simple filling worked in small straight stitches of equal size placed at random within a design area.

French knot Bring out thread and pull it through completely. Hold needle in left hand and place it to the left of the point of exit of the thread; the needle should point toward you. Take thread in your right hand at the point closest to the fabric and bring it over and under the needle. Without releasing the thread, bring the needle to an upright position and reinsert it into the fabric right next to (but not into) the original point of exit. Pull the needle slowly with your left hand until the entire thread is almost pulled through, and release right hand. The knot should sit firmly on top of the fabric and have a little dimple in the center. For a heavier knot use heavier thread but don't twist thread around needle more than once.

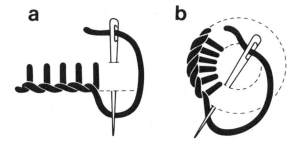

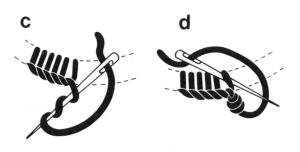

Buttonhole stitch   Bring the needle out on the lower line to the left of the work. Insert the needle in the upper line and take a straight stitch downward. Hold thread with left thumb and guide the needle over it and repeat. When the stitches are worked very close you have a buttonhole stitch. When they are worked wide apart you have a blanket stitch.

Buttonhole stitch is durable and may be worked around eyelet holes instead of overcasting.

Buttonhole with picot   A decorative picot may be worked in with the buttonhole stitch to create an attractive border. Work several buttonhole stitches, then wind the thread around the needle, pull it through into a knot, bring needle under the last stitch and over the thread, and pull again. Repeat. Place picots at equal intervals.

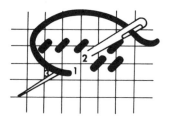

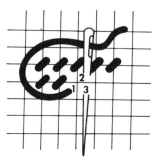

Continental stitch   A half cross-stitch used in canvas work. Use a blunt tapestry needle and work from right to left across the crossover point of the canvas mesh. At the end of the line, turn the work over and stitch again from left to right. This version of the half cross-stitch has a tendency to distort the finished canvas and will require blocking.

Half cross-stitch   Work the first line in continental stitch but don't turn the canvas over on the return row. Hold it in the same position and work from left to right, as indicated in the diagram. This stitch technique works best on a double-mesh canvas. There is not as much distortion as in continental stitch but the line worked from left to right looks different from the one worked from right to left, forming ridges. This is sometimes very effective on a plain background. See the photograph of the rug on page 23.

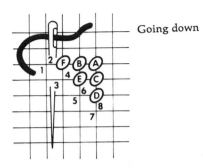

Going down

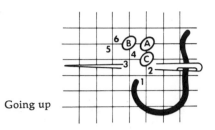

Going up

Basketweave stitch So named because of the manner in which it is worked, this stitch creates an interwoven or basketweave effect on the wrong side of the canvas. Begin in the upper right-hand corner at *A*, then work *B* and come down to *C* under *A*. Work another stitch under *C* and proceed upward, 1–2, 3–4, 5–6. The needle is always used horizontally when working up. Basketweave stitching is worked diagonally; when the row is stitched downward, the needle is vertical. Practice this stitch before attempting a large project. There is very little distortion in basketweave.

The **Ghiordes knot** may be used as a fringe border.

A

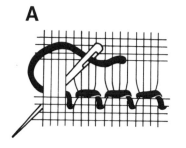

B

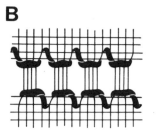

Hemstitch This is the basic stitch in drawnwork and is used in preparation to needleweaving. Establish the length and width of your border. Withdraw the top and bottom thread across the width of your fabric. This will indicate the width of your hemstitch border. Work a fine buttonhole stitch across the vertical line between the drawn threads. Do this at each end of the border. Clip the horizontal threads of the fabric along the buttonhole stitch lines. Be careful not to cut the vertical threads. Pull out the horizontal threads between the two you drew out at the beginning. Draw them out carefully, one at a time.

Work the hemstitch tightly from right to left, as indicated in the diagram. Tie two or more of the exposed vertical threads in even bunches. Turn your work around and repeat hemstitching on the reverse side (*B*). A narrow hemstitched border is very attractive when worked around table linens.

A

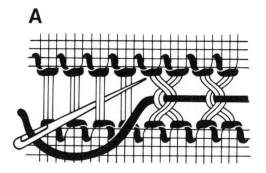

B

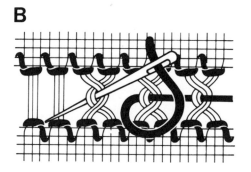

Interlaced hemstitch Work hemstitch on both sides as just described. Fasten a long thread at the right-hand side of the work and through the center of the buttonhole stitch bar. Bring the working thread over the first two groups of tied threads and insert the needle from left to right as indicated in the diagram. Twist the left group of threads over the right one and pull the needle through. Pull thread firmly as you work, and when you reach the other end of the border fasten it to the center of that buttonhole edge.

177

LIST OF SUPPLIERS

Wholesale distributors

As a courtesy to the dealer, please send a stamped, self-addressed envelope with your inquiries.

Art Needlework
Treasure Trove
P.O. Box 2440
Grand Central Station
New York, N.Y. 10017

Canvas (interlocked and conventional), D.M.C. yarns, Aida cloth and other embroidery fabrics, Marlit rayon, counted-thread books

Paternayan Brothers
312 East 95 St.
New York, N.Y. 10028

Paterna Persian yarn, Pat rug yarn, needles, white and brown needlepoint canvas, Rya cloth, crewel yarn

Handwork Tapestries
P.O. Box 54
Baldwin, N.Y. 11510

Laine Colbert tapestry yarn, Colbert 6 Smyrne rug yarn, Medicis crewel yarn, silk threads, needlepoint canvas, and counted-thread Aida and Hardanger cloth

O. Oehlenschlagers
EFTR. A/S
Drejogade 11
2100 Kopenhagen 0
Denmark

Even-weave linens and cottons and canvas in a large assortment of gauges and colors; tapestry wool yarn suitable for counted-thread cross-stitch, counted-stitch patterns; stamped canvas and linen

Carl J. Permin A/S
Ny Ostergade 3
1101 Kopenhagen K
Denmark

Even-weave linens and cottons in a large assortment of colors and gauges; tapestry wool yarn suitable for counted-thread cross-stitch and counted-stitch patterns; stamped canvas and linen

Thumbelina Needlework
Shop
1685 Copenhagen Dr.
Solvang, Calif. 93463

Danish imports

Swedish Style Gift Shop 5209 North Clark Chicago, Ill. 60640	Danish imports
Walbead 38 West 37th St. New York, N.Y. 10018	Beads, sequins, etc., wholesale and retail; will mail catalogue
Clara Waever 42 Ostergade 1100 Copenhagen K Denmark	Beads, sequins, etc., wholesale and retail; will mail catalogue
JES Handicrafts P.O. Box 341 Closter, N.J. 07624	Darning net and mercerized cotton for needle-weaving
George Wells The Ruggery 565 Cedar Swamp Rd. Glen Head, Long Island, N.Y. 11545	Rug yarn, dyes, linen, canvas

BIBLIOGRAPHY

Arnold, Bruce. *A Concise History of Irish Art.*
    London: Thames and Hudson, 1969.

Bain, George. *Celtic Art.*
    New York: Dover Publications, 1973.

Caulfield, S. F. A., and Saward, B. C. *Dictionary of Needlework.*
    New York: Arno Press, 1972. (Reprinted)

Christie, Mrs. Archibald. *Samplers and Stitches.*
    New York: E. P. Dutton Co., 1920.

Durant, Will. *Our Oriental Heritage.*
    New York: Simon & Schuster, 1954.

Horsia, Olga, and Petrescu, Paul. *Artistic Handicrafts in Romania.*
    Bucharest, Romania: Central Union of Handicraft Cooperatives, 1972.

In the Land of the Reindeer.
    Leningrad: Aurora Art Publishers, 1974.

Kiadás, Második. *Kalocsa Népmüvészete (The Folk Art of Kalocsa).*
    Kalocsa, Hungary: Kalocsa Város Tanácsa V. B., 1973.

Wardle, Patricia. *Guide to English Embroidery.*
    London: Victoria and Albert Museum, 1970.